Questions in
Intermediate 2
Maths

Ken Nisbet

Text © 2006 Ken Nisbet
Design & layout © 2006 Leckie & Leckie
Cover image © Dr Seth Shostak/Science Photo Library

1st Edition 2006

All rights reserved. No part of this publication may be reproduced, stored in a retrieval system, or transmitted in any form or by any means, electronic, mechanical, photocopying, recording or otherwise, without prior permission in writing from Leckie & Leckie Ltd. Legal action will be taken by Leckie & Leckie Ltd against any infringement of our copyright.

The right of Ken Nisbet to be identified as the author of this Work has been asserted by him in accordance with sections 77 and 78 of the Copyright, Designs and Patents Act 1988.

ISBN 1-84372-148-1
ISBN-13 978-1-84372-148-2

Published by
Leckie & Leckie Ltd, 3rd floor, 4 Queen Street, Edinburgh, EH2 1JF
Tel: 0131 220 6831 Fax: 0131 225 9987
enquiries@leckieandleckie.co.uk   www.leckieandleckie.co.uk

Special thanks to
BRW (creative packaging), Pumpkin House (creative design), River Design (cover design),
Caleb O'Loan (content checking), Robin Waterston (content review), Tara Watson (proofreading).

A CIP catalogue record for this book is available from the British Library.

Leckie & Leckie Ltd is a division of Granada Learning Limited.

Contents

Introduction

Skills and Techniques Revision

Unit 1   **6**
- 1   Percentages and Significant Figures   6
- 2   Volumes of Solids   9
- 3   Linear Relationships   13
- 4   Algebraic Operations   16
- 5   Circles   19

Unit 2   **24**
- 6   Trigonometry   24
- 7   Simultaneous Linear Equations   29
- 8   Graphs, Charts and Tables   31
- 9   Statistics   35

Unit 3   **40**
- 10   Further Algebraic Operations   40
- 11   Quadratic Graphs and Equations   44
- 12   Further Trigonometry   48

Exam Structure and Formulae   **52**

Unit Assessments   **53**
- Practice Assessment A for Unit 1   54
- Practice Assessment B for Unit 1   56
- Practice Assessment A for Unit 2   58
- Practice Assessment B for Unit 2   60
- Practice Assessment A for Unit 3   62
- Practice Assessment B for Unit 3   64

Course Assessments   **66**
- Practice Exam A Paper 1   67
- Practice Exam A Paper 2   68
- Practice Exam B Paper 1   70
- Practice Exam B Paper 2   71

Answers   **pull-out section**

Introduction

What this book contains

There are four sections in this Question Book:

- **Skills and Techniques Revision**

    This is a bank of questions designed to help you develop your skills and techniques in maths to a level where you will achieve success in examination questions. The skills and techniques concentrated on are those that occur most frequently in the exam.

- **Unit Assessments**

    This section contains Revision Exercises which focus on each outcome of each Unit Assessment (NAB). They may be used either for pratice before your Assessment or for focussed preparation for a resit of a particular outcome. Sample Unit Assessments are also provided for you to practise in preparation for your Unit Assessment.

- **Course Assessments**

    Two complete Exams are provided. They have similar content, structure and difficulty range to the exams you will be sitting.

- **Answers and Solutions**

    This section contains:

    The answers to the revision exercises in the Skills and Techniques section

    The answers to the revision exercises in the Unit Assessment section

    Full solutions to the Practice Unit Assessments

    Full solutions to the Practice Course Exam A and Exam B

Leckie & Leckie's Intermediate 2 Maths Revision Notes

Questions in Intermediate 2 Maths is the companion volume to Leckie & Leckie's *Intermediate 2 Maths Revision Notes*. We recommend that you work with both books when revising for your exam. You will find extensive cross-references between the illustrative worked examples in the Revision Notes and the corresponding Revision Exercises in the Questions. Where you see the following book symbol beside a question, it will contain the number of the relevant worked example from the Revision Notes.

Suggestions for using this book

There are many ways of using the revision material in this book. We recommend the following focused system:

Step 1: Sit Practice Exam A as a timed exercise.

Step 2: Compare your attempted solutions with the full solutions provided to identify your weak areas.

Step 3: Use the Skills and Techniques Revision Exercises to strengthen those weak areas.

Step 4: After completing Steps 1–3 wait a few days and then repeat Steps 1–3 using Exam B. It is this repetitive practice of problems that will improve your chances of achieving a good grade in the final exam.
In preparation for sitting your Unit Assessments (NABs) likewise follow a similar system using the Practice Unit Assessments and Unit Assessment Revision Exercises.

Additional Comments

There is a wide range of difficulty in the Exercises in the Skills and Techniques section. If you devote enough time and effort to these exercises you will eventually master the skills and techniques that you need. A lot depends on your own belief that you can eventually succeed. Practice does make perfect. It is not possible in a book of this nature to cover all the material that is likely to occur in your exam and it is therefore vital that you attempt as many of the actual Past Papers as you can. Best wishes for success in your Intermediate 2 Maths Exam and we hope that our revision books will help you towards this success.

Formulae

You will be given the following formulae in all assessments.

The roots of $ax^2 + bx + c = 0$ are $x = \dfrac{-b \pm \sqrt{(b^2 - 4ac)}}{2a}$

Sine rule: $\dfrac{a}{\sin A} = \dfrac{b}{\sin B} = \dfrac{c}{\sin C}$

Cosine rule: $a^2 = b^2 + c^2 - 2bc \cos A$ or $\cos A = \dfrac{b^2 + c^2 - a^2}{2bc}$

Area of a triangle: Area $= \tfrac{1}{2} ab \sin C$

Volume of a sphere: Volume $= \tfrac{4}{3} \pi r^3$

Volume of a cone: Volume $= \tfrac{1}{3} \pi r^2 h$

Volume of a cylinder: Volume $= \pi r^2 h$

Standard deviation: $s = \sqrt{\dfrac{\sum(x - \bar{x})^2}{n - 1}} = \sqrt{\dfrac{\sum x^2 - (\sum x)^2 / n}{n - 1}}$, where n is the sample size

Skills and Techniques Revision

1 Percentages and significant figures

1.3

Exercise 1a Rounding Measurements

1 The following are calculator displays. Round them to (i) 3 significant figures (ii) 2 significant figures (iii) 1 significant figure.

- a 38·6847328
- b 572·439216
- c 1327·12579
- d 25·5583924
- e 650·597213
- f 4585·29938
- g 0·62394721
- h 0·15592361
- i 0·83568754

2 Round these numbers as indicated:

- a 23·85 to 1 decimal place
- b 0·863 to 1 decimal place
- c £13823·50 to the nearest thousand pounds
- d £2450 to the nearest hundred pounds
- e 8253 m to the nearest thousand metres
- f 255·9 kg to the nearest ten kilograms

1.4

Exercise 1b Finding a % of a Quantity

1 VAT (Value Added Tax) is charged at 17·5%. Find, to the nearest penny, the VAT added to a bill of:

- a £34
- b £240
- c £37·60
- d £145·50
- e £1230
- f £2845·30

2 For each loan calculate the interest charged:

- a £1000 for 1 year at 12·5% per annum
- b £550 for 6 months at 18% per annum
- c £380 for 1 month at 1·8% per month
- d £1200 for 1 month at 1·2% per month
- e £2600 for 4 months at 14·5% per annum

3 Which of these two loans charges more interest
£800 for 3 months at 8·5% per annum
£1000 for 4 months at 5·4% per annum?

1.5

Exercise 1c Expressing one Quantity as a % of another Quantity

1 The following are price increases or decreases. In each case calculate the % increase or decrease, giving your answer to 1 decimal place:

- a 42p to 45p
- b 95p to 90p
- c £5·30 to £5·85
- d £8·30 to £7·90
- e £122 to £120
- f £380 to £390
- g £28·12 to £31·59
- h £1350 to £1220

See pages 3–6 of Leckie & Leckie's Intermediate 2 Maths Revision Notes

1 Percentages and significant figures

2 The table shows how the values of three houses increased from June to August. Which house had the greatest percentage increase?

	June	August
House A	£135000	£137700
House B	£220000	£223300
House C	£95000	£97375

Exercise 1d Appreciation and Depreciation

1 Use a multiplier to:

a increase £340 by 12%
b decrease £500 by 6%
c decrease £1250 by 8%
d increase £23 by 15%
e increase £15000 by 9%
f decrease £18400 by 5·5%

2 a The population of Tadworth is 48000 and is increasing at a steady rate of 3·6% per annum. What is the expected population in 4 years time? Give your answer to the nearest thousand.

b A patient at 10am has 800 mg of a drug in her blood. If the amount of the drug reduces by 5% each hour, how many mg are in her blood by 1pm?

c A house is worth £185000 in 2007. If its value rises at a rate of 3% per year, what would its value be in 2010? Give your answer to the nearest thousand pounds.

d The gardener left a greenhouse window open causing the temperature to drop by 4% each hour. If he did this at 7pm when the temperature was 32°C, what was the temperature in the greenhouse by 10pm? Give your answer to the nearest degree.

e In Banff house prices are expected to rise by 1·8% per month. What would be the expected value of a house worth £115000 after a further 3 months? Give your answer to three significant figures.

3 a House prices in Fife are expected to rise by 2·5% per month and those in the Borders by 1·5% per month. How many months would it take until a house in Fife valued at £175000 has a greater value than a house in the Borders valued at £180000?

b Culture A has 15000 bacteria and is increasing at a steady rate of 16% per hour. Culture B has 35000 bacteria and is decreasing at a steady rate of 13% per hour. How many hours will it be before Culture A has more bacteria than Culture B?

See Answers on page 1 of answer booklet

1 Percentages and significant figures

Exercise 1e Compound Interest

1. Calculate (i) the final amount (ii) the compound interest for the following investments:
   a. £400 for 3 years at 4% p.a.
   b. £1200 for 2 years at $6\frac{1}{2}$ % p.a.
   c. £50000 for 4 years at 20% p.a.
   d. £8800 for 2 years at $12\frac{1}{2}$ % p.a.

2. Find the cost (i.e. the interest charged) of the following loans giving your answer to the nearest penny where necessary:
   a. £2000 for 3 months at 1·8% per month
   b. £560 for 4 months at 0·9% per month
   c. £12000 for 2 months at 2·5% per month
   d. £85000 for 6 months at 1·5% per month

3. Iain wishes to borrow £2000 for 4 months. He can choose from Loanhelp whose interest rate is 1·3% per month or Largeloan who charge 16·5% per annum. Which Loan Company costs less?

Exercise 1f Further Percentage Calculations

1. In each case calculate the original price before the increase or decrease:
   a. £246·75 after an increase of 5%
   b. £258·16 after an increase of 12%
   c. £81·32 after a decrease of 5%
   d. £1337·60 after a decrease of 12%
   e. £103·32 after a decrease of 18%
   f. £53·30 after an increase of $2\frac{1}{2}$%

2. The following prices were all the result of a year where the price inflation rate was 2·4%. What was each price at the start of the year?
   a. £25·60
   b. £122·88
   c. £1536
   d. £12339·20

2 Volumes of solids   UNIT 1

2.2 Exercise 2a Spheres

1. Find the volume of a sphere with radius (giving your answers to 2 significant figures):

   a 0·4 cm   b 1·2 cm   c 9·8 cm

   d 20 cm   e 0·15 cm

2. Paperweights are made in the shape of a hemisphere. Find the volume of glass required to make a paperweight with radius:

   a 3 cm   b 4 cm

   c 3·6 cm   d 2·9 cm

   (Give answers to 3 significant figures.)

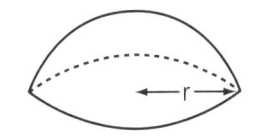

3. A slab of chocolate in the shape of a cuboid with dimensions 9 cm × 3·2 cm × 1·9 cm is melted and made into small spherical sweets with radius 0·2 cm. How many sweets can be made?

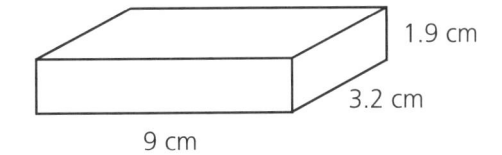

2.3 Exercise 2b Cones

1. Without using a calculator find to 1 significant figure the volumes of the following cones. Use π = 3·14.

   a $r = 1$ cm, $h = 30$ cm   b $r = 3$ cm, $h = 10$ cm

   c $r = 10$ cm, $h = 12$ cm   d $r = 0·3$ cm, $h = 100$ cm

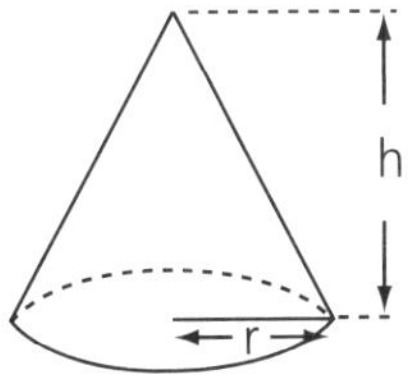

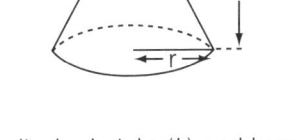

2. Find, to 3 significant figures, the volume of a cone with perpendicular height (h) and base radius (r) as given:

   a $h = 4$ cm, $r = 3$ cm   b $h = 7·3$ cm, $r = 4$ cm

   c $h = 0·8$ m, $r = 1·2$ m   d $h = 54$ cm, $r = 23$ cm

3. Frustum Ices use containers in the shape of part of a cone as shown. Calculate the volume of each container shown below giving your answers to 2 significant figures:

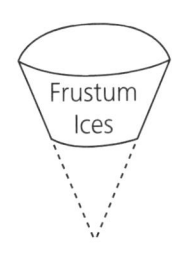

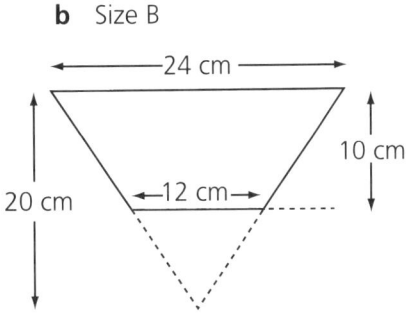

   a Size A: top 18 cm, middle 12 cm, height 7 cm, total 21 cm

   b Size B: top 24 cm, middle 12 cm, height 10 cm, total 20 cm

   c Size C: top 15 cm, middle 9 cm, height 8 cm, total 20 cm

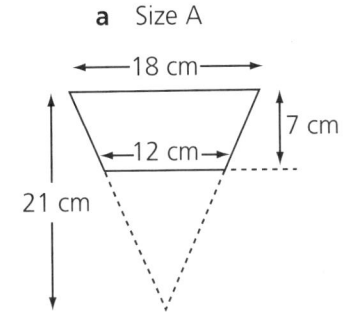

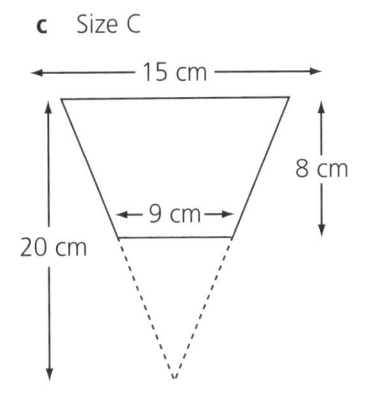

2 Volumes of solids

Exercise 2c Prisms

1. Find, to 2 significant figures, the volume of a cylinder with height (h) and base radius (r) as given:

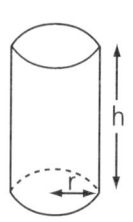

   a h = 10 cm, r = 2 cm   **b** h = 12·6 cm, r = 4·8 cm

   c h = 3·6 cm, r = 0·8 cm   **d** h = 123 cm, r = 47 cm

2. A 10 cm wide strip of metal is cut into different lengths. Each length is rolled to form the cylindrical wall of a can. Calculate, correct to 2 significant figures, the volume of each can if the radius of the base is:

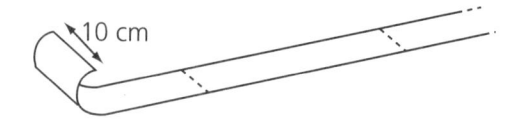

   a 2 cm   **b** 2·5 cm   **c** 3 cm   **d** 3·5 cm

3. For each of these prisms calculate its volume giving your answer to two significant figures:

   a 16 cm, 12 cm — Semi-circular end

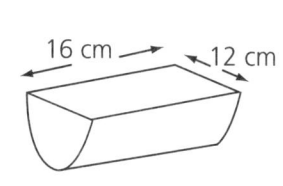

   b 2 m, 2·2 m, 3·5 m — Triangular end with vertical height 2m

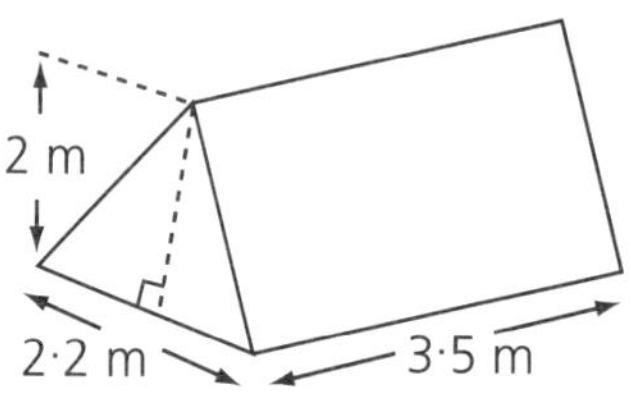

   c 28 cm, 20 cm, 10 cm — Top is in shape of a rectangle with two semi-circles

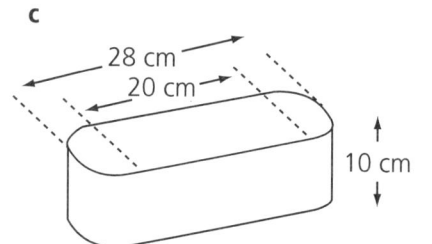

   d 8 m, 13 m, 5 m, 10 m — The end is in the shape of a rectangle surmounted by an isosceles triangle.

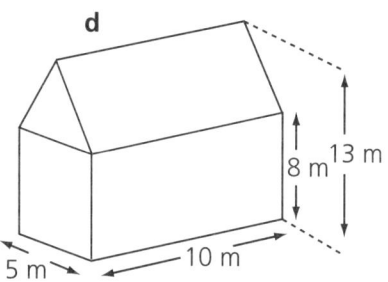

   e 10 m, 26 m, 30 m — The end is in the shape of a rectangle surmounted by a semi-circle.

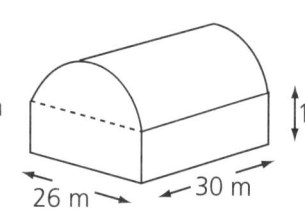

   f 28 cm, 15 cm, 21 cm — The end is in the shape of a rectangle and a quarter-circle.

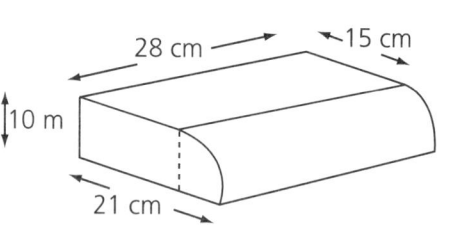

Exercise 2d Composite Solids

1. Find, to 3 significant figures, the volume of these solids:

   a 10 cm, 12 cm — A cone surmounted by a hemisphere

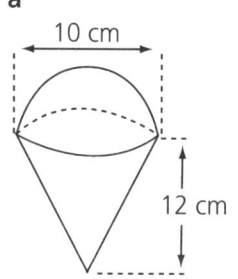

   b 12 cm, 36 cm — A cylinder with a hemisphere on each end

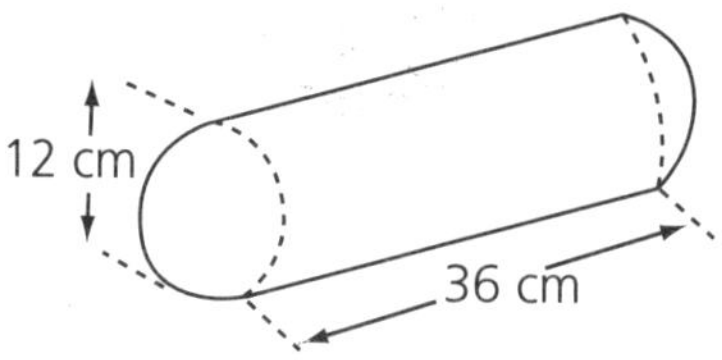

See pages 7–8 of Leckie & Leckie's Intermediate 2 Maths Revision Notes

2 Volumes of solids — UNIT 1

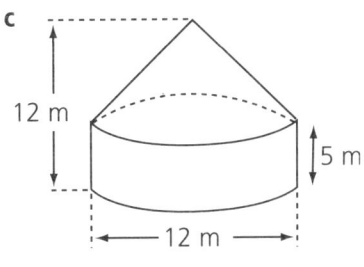

c 12 m, 5 m, 12 m
A cylinder surmounted by a cone

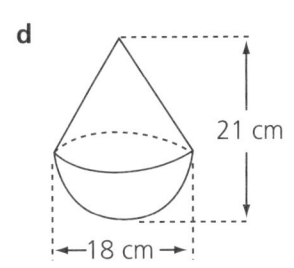

d 21 cm, 18 cm
A hemisphere surmounted by a cone

2 The design for a small chapel is shown. It consists of a cuboid surmounted by a triangular prism with cross-section in the shape of an isosceles triangle. On one end is attached half a cylinder surmounted by half a cone.

The chapel is designed to seat 20 people but regulations state that each person should have 80 m³ of air. Does this design meet regulations?

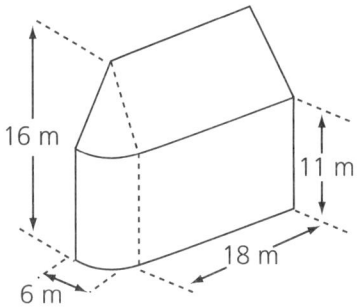

16 m, 11 m, 18 m, 6 m

Exercise 2e Missing Lengths

1 For each solid find the missing length. Give answers to 2 significant figures where necessary:

a a triangular prism
8 m, x m, 15 m
volume = 360 m³

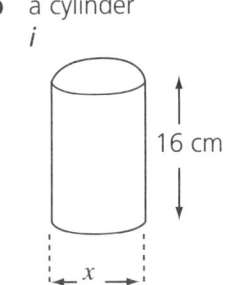

b a cylinder

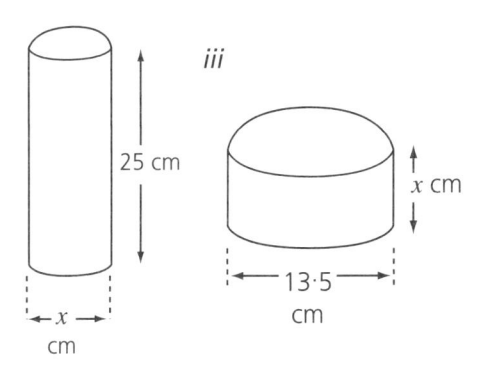

i 16 cm, x cm
volume = 450 cm³

ii 25 cm, x cm
volume = 250 cm³

iii 13·5 cm, x cm
volume = 430 cm³

2 This tent is shaped as a triangular prism with base area a 2 m × 5 m rectangle and height 3 m.

a Calculate the volume of the tent.

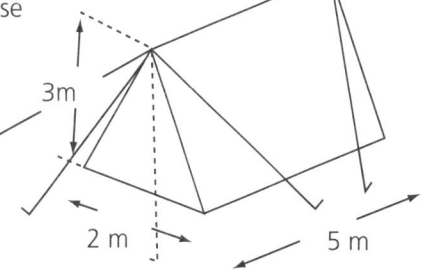

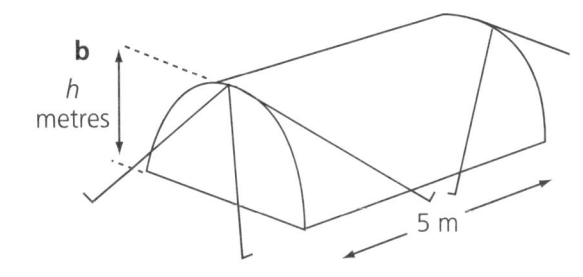

3 m, 2 m, 5 m

b h metres, 5 m

The tent is redesigned to form a prism with semi-circular end. If it has the same length (5 m) and the same volume, calculate, to three significant figures, its height.

See Answers on pages 1–2 of answer booklet

2 Volumes of solids

3 Find the height of each cone. Give your answer correct to two significant figures..

a 6 cm (base radius), volume = 500 cm³

b 8 cm (base diameter), volume = 500 cm³

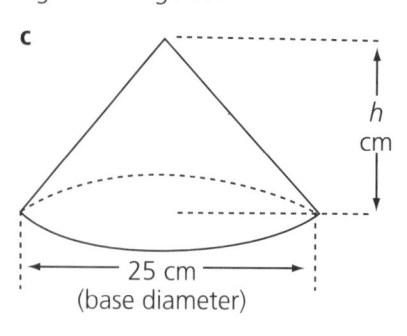

c 25 cm (base diameter), volume = 5400 cm³

4 Chillip Ice Cream arrives at the shop in cylindrical containers with dimensions as shown. They are then sold as ice cream cones with radius 2·5 cm as shown. 450 such cones can be filled using 1 container.

(Cylinder: 30 cm height, 20 cm diameter. Cone: 2·5 cm radius)

  a Calculate, to three significant figures, the volume of one container.

  b Calculate, to two significant figures, the height of a cone.

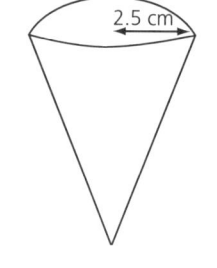

5 One large cylindrical cheese with dimensions as shown is broken down and packed into small wedges.

(Cylinder: 25 cm height, 35 cm diameter. Cheese wedge: 2 cm thick)

Each wedge is 2 cm thick and has a uniform cross-section that is a quarter of a circle.

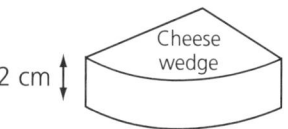

If 1200 wedges can be made from one large cheese, calculate the radius of the cross-section of the wedge. Give your answer to two significant figures.

6 Helium gas is stored in a cylinder with radius 12 cm. When released it fills a volume 1500 times greater than the volume of the cylinder. One cylinder fills a spherical balloon of radius 2·5 m. Calculate the length of one cylinder to two significant figures.

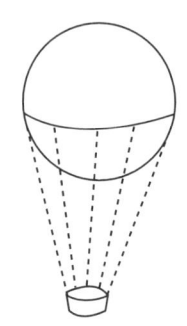

See pages 7–8 of Leckie & Leckie's Intermediate 2 Maths Revision Notes

3 Linear relationships

UNIT 1

3.1 Exercise 3a What is Gradient?

Give the gradients of the following lines:

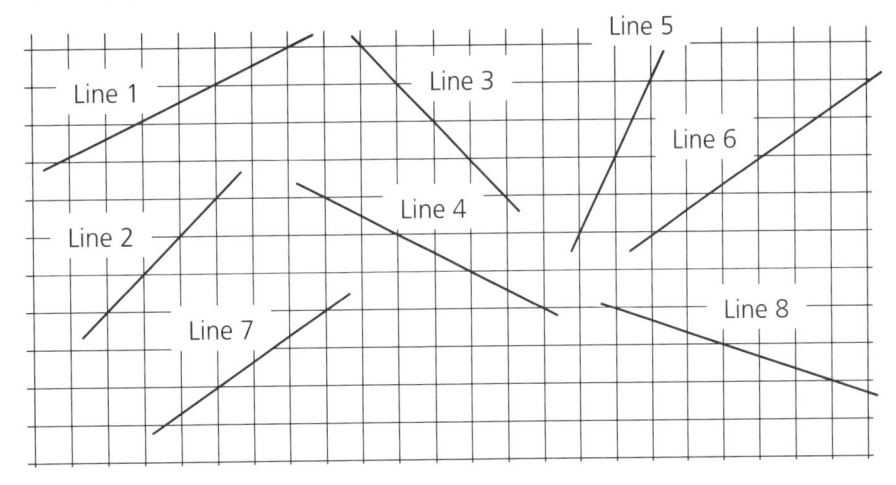

(Lines 1–8 shown on grid)

3.2 Exercise 3b Gradient Formula

Calculate the gradient of the line AB for:

1. A(6, 2) and B(4, 0)
2. A(3, 7) and B(0, 1)
3. A(4, 1) and B(7, −8)
4. A(−1, −1) and B(3, 1)
5. A(6, 3) and B(−4, 8)
6. A(−10, −2) and B(−1, 4)
7. A(7, −9) and B(−1, −3)
8. A(−11, −2) and B(−3, 10)
9. A(−17, 3) and B(−2, −2)

3.3 Exercise 3c Graphs from Equations

1. Draw straight line graphs for the following equations:

   a. $y = 2x - 1$
   b. $y = x + 3$
   c. $y = -2x + 1$
   d. $y = -x + 2$
   e. $y = \frac{1}{2}x + 2$
   f. $y = -\frac{1}{2}x + 1$
   g. $y = x + 8$
   h. $y + 2x = 6$
   i. $y = -\frac{2}{3}x + 5$

2. Find the coordinates of the point where the two lines with the given equations meet:

   a. $y = x$ and $y = -2x + 3$
   b. $y = 3x$ and $y = -\frac{1}{2}x + 7$

3.4 Exercise 3d Equations from Graphs

1. Find the equations of these straight lines:

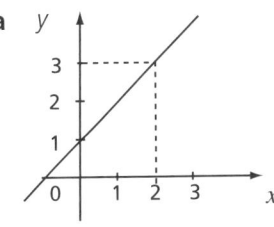

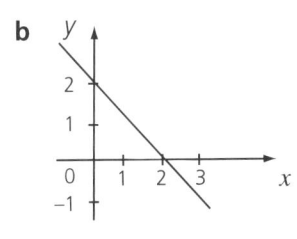

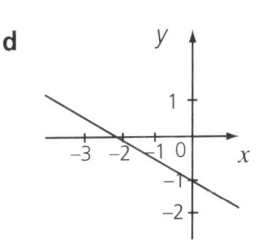

   a, b, c, d (graphs shown)

See Answers on page 2 of answer booklet

UNIT 1

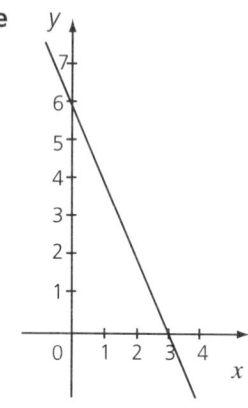

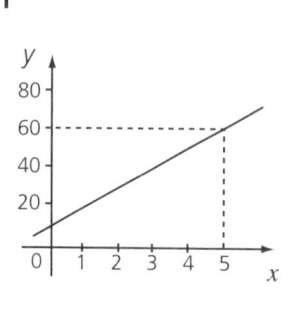

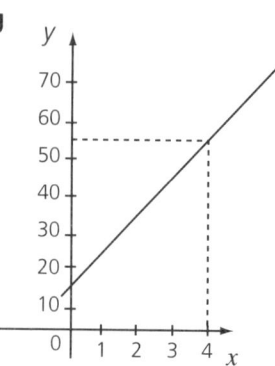

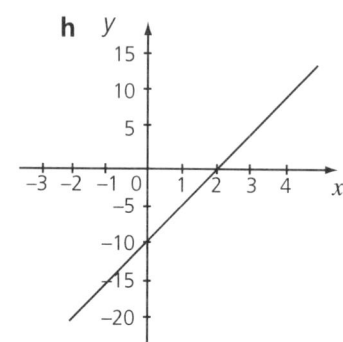

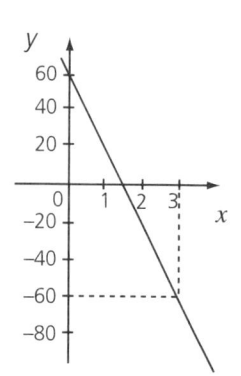

3 Linear relationships

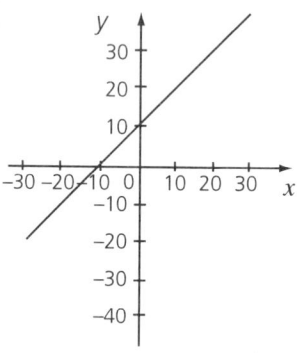

2 Find the equations of these straight lines:

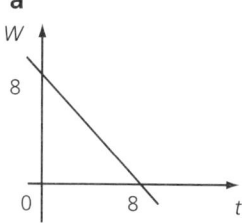

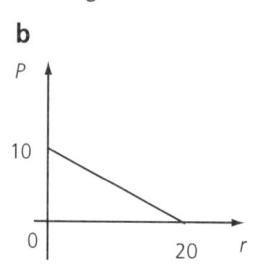

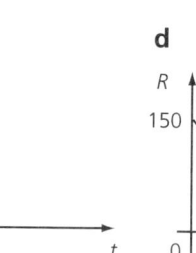

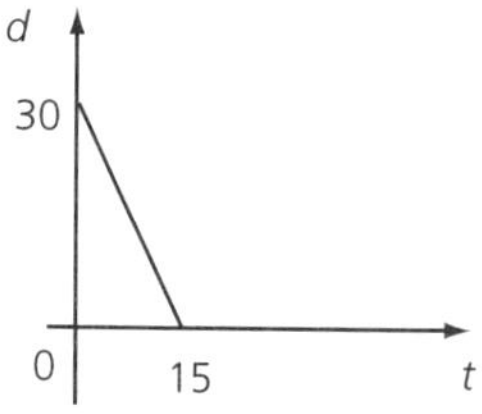

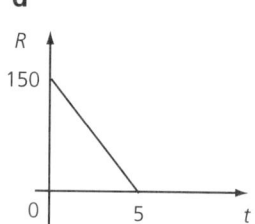

3 a The temperature of a liquid started at 80°C. It fell at a steady rate of 10°C per minute. The graph of the temperature, T°C, of the liquid against the time, t minutes, is shown in the diagram.

Write down an equation connecting T and t.

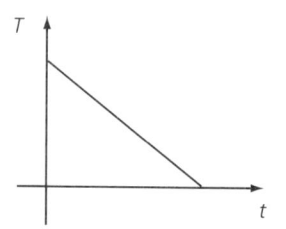

b A petrol tanker containing 15000 litres of petrol arrives at a garage. It unloads petrol at a steady rate of 500 litres per minute until it is empty. The graph of the amount of petrol in the tanker, L litres, against the time, t minutes, is shown in the diagram.

Write down an equation connecting L and t.

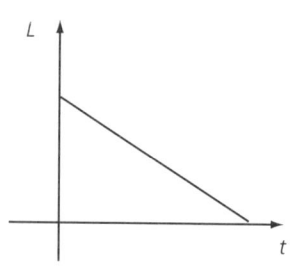

See pages 9–12 of Leckie & Leckie's Intermediate 2 Maths Revision Notes

3 Linear relationships

UNIT 1

4 The graph represents the distance (*d* km) to Edinburgh against the time (*t* hours) from the start of a train's journey.

   a Find the equation of the line in terms of *d* and *t*.

   b How long does it take the train to travel 50 km?

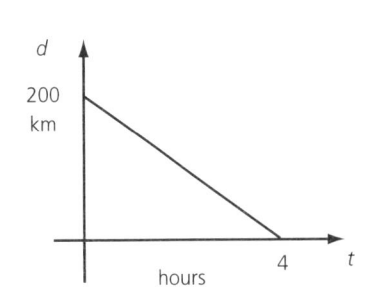

Exercise 3e Axes Intercepts

For each straight line equation find the co-ordinates of the point where it crosses

   a the *y*-axis   **b** the *x*-axis.

1 $y = 3x - 6$ **2** $y + 2x = 4$ **3** $y - 5x = 10$

4 $2y + 3x = 6$ **5** $3y = 12 - 2x$ **6** $4y = 12x - 12$

7 $4y - 3x = 4$ **8** $5y + 2x = 4$ **9** $3y - 4x - 6 = 0$

Exercise 3f What's the Point?

In each case determine which of the three points lie on the line with the given equation:

1 A(2, 4),   B(–1, 7),   C(8, –3)   ; $x + y = 6$

2 D(1, –1),   E(–1, 1),   F(5, 7)   ; $2x - y = 3$

3 K(8, 0),   L(10, 3),   M(–6, –5)   ; $y = \frac{1}{2}x - 2$

4 N(–3, 2),   P(1, 4),   Q(–9, –2)   ; $3y - 2x = 12$

Exercise 3g Parallel Lines

In each case determine which (if any!) of the three lines are parallel. (Parallel lines have equal gradients.)

1 **a** $y = 3x - 2$ **b** $3y = x + 6$ **c** $y - 3x = 4$

2 **a** $y = x - 1$ **b** $y - 2x = 1$ **c** $y - 3x = 1$

3 **a** $6y = 3x + 2$ **b** $2y = x$ **c** $2y - x = 6$

4 **a** $2y + x = 1$ **b** $2y + 2x = 1$ **c** $2y + x = -2$

4 Algebraic operations

4.1

Exercise 4a Adding, Subtracting and Multiplying Terms

1 Simplify:

    a $4x^2 - x + 3x - 1 + 2x - 3x^2$ **b** $5 + 2x - x + x^2 - 3 - 4x^2$

    c $2y + x^2 - 3x - y + 4x - 2x^2$ **d** $12y^2 - 3x^2 - x^2 + 2y^2$

    e $3x + 1 + 3x + 1 + x - 2 + x - 2$ **f** $6x^3 - 3x^2 - 8x^3 + 2x + 3x^2 - 2x$

2 Find an expression for the perimeter of each of these shapes:

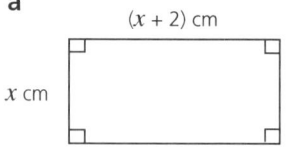

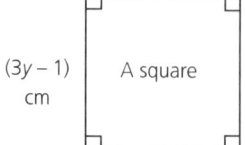

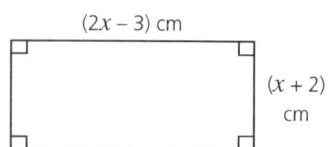

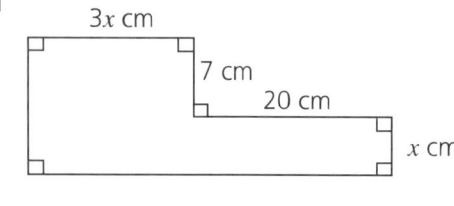

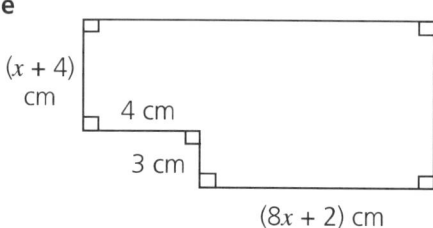

a rectangle: $(x + 2)$ cm by x cm

b A square with side $(3y - 1)$ cm

c rectangle: $(2x - 3)$ cm by $(x + 2)$ cm

d L-shape with sides $3x$ cm, 7 cm, 20 cm, x cm

e L-shape with sides $(x + 4)$ cm, 4 cm, 3 cm, $(8x + 2)$ cm

3 Simplify:

    a $x - (-3x)$ **b** $-2x - 3x$ **c** $x \times 2y$

    d $3x \times 2x$ **e** $(2x)^2$ **f** $3x^2 \times 5x$

    g $2a \times 7b$ **h** $3ab - 5ab$ **i** $a \times (-b) \times a$

    j $-5x \times (-3x)$ **k** $-5x - (-3x)$ **l** $-2a \times (-a) - 2a^2$

4.2

Exercise 4b Removing One Pair of Brackets

1 Simplify:

    a $3(x - 2)$ **b** $-2(x + 3)$ **c** $2(5 - y)$

    d $-(x - 2)$ **e** $-5(2x - 3)$ **f** $-3(5 - 2x)$

    g $4(x^2 - 3x)$ **h** $-(2x - 5x^2)$

2 Simplify by removing brackets and collecting like terms:

    a $6(4x - 2) - 3(2x + 3)$ **b** $2(3y + 1) - 4(2y - 3)$

    c $x(3x - 1) - 2x(x + 4)$ **d** $3x(4x - 2) - 2x(3x - 2)$

    e $a(3b + 2) + b(2a - 1)$ **f** $5y(3 + 2y) - 2y(4y - 1)$

See pages 12–17 of Leckie & Leckie's Intermediate 2 Maths Revision Notes

4 Algebraic operations

Exercise 4c Removing Two Pairs of Brackets

1 Simplify:

a $(x - 2)(x + 3)$ b $(2x + 1)(3x - 2)$ c $(3a - 2)(a + 5)$

d $(5x - 1)(3x + 2)$ e $(3x - 2)(3x - 1)$ f $(x - 8)(2x - 3)$

g $(x - y)(x + y)$ h $(3a - b)(2a + 3b)$ i $(5x - 2y)(x - 3y)$

2 Multiply out the brackets and collect like terms:

a $(2x + 3)(x - 1) + 3x$ b $4x + (x - 3)(2x + 5)$

c $(3a - 2)(a - 1) - a^2$ d $(3x + 4)(x - 2) + 5x^2 - x$

e $x - (x + 2)(x + 3)$ f $3x^2 - (2x - 1)(x + 5)$

3 a Write down expressions for the areas of these two rectangles:

Rectangle I: $(x + 2)$ cm by $(x + 3)$ cm

Rectangle II: $(x + 1)$ cm by $(x + 4)$ cm

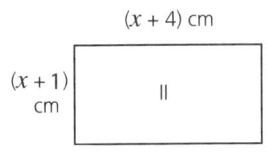

b The area of rectangle I is greater than the area of rectangle II. By how much is it greater?

Exercise 4d Brackets Squared

Multiply out the brackets and collect like terms:

1 $(2x - 1)^2$ **2** $(3x + 2)^2$ **3** $(a - 2b)^2$

4 $(2x + y)^2$ **5** $(x + 3)^2 - 2x$ **6** $(2x - 4)^2 + x^2$

7 $3x^2 + (4x - 1)^2$ **8** $5x - (x - 2)^2$ **9** $(x + 1)^2 - (x - 1)^2$

10 $(2a - b)^2 - (2a + b)^2$

Exercise 4e Larger Brackets

Multiply out the brackets and collect like terms:

1 $(x + 1)(x^2 + 2x - 1)$ **2** $(x + 3)(2x^2 - x + 2)$ **3** $(x - 2)(x^2 - 2x + 1)$

4 $(x - 3)(x^2 + 3x - 2)$ **5** $(2x + 1)(x^2 - x - 1)$ **6** $(2x - 1)(2x^2 + x - 3)$

7 $(x - 5)(x^2 + 3x - 2)$ **8** $(2 - x)(1 - 3x + x^2)$

Exercise 4f Common Factors

Factorise completely:

1 $4y^2 + 8y$ **2** $3x^2 - 12x$ **3** $5a^2 + 10a$

4 $2ab + 4ac$ **5** $12x - 8x^2$ **6** $4ab - 2b^2$

7 $14b - 21b^2$ **8** $6a^2 + 8ab$ **9** $ab^2 - a^2b$

10 $6m^2 - 18mn$ **11** $24x^2 - 32x^3$ **12** $4y^2 + 12y^3$

4 Algebraic operations

Exercise 4g Difference of Two Squares

Factorise:

1. $25x^2 - 9y^2$
2. $4a^2 - 25b^2$
3. $x^2 - 49$
4. $100 - 4x^2$
5. $4 - 16a^2$
6. $9m^2 - 16n^2$
7. $64x^2 - 9y^2$
8. $81x^2 - 121$
9. $36a^2 - 25b^2$
10. $4m^2 - 900$
11. $400 - 49y^2$
12. $121x^2 - 144y^2$

Exercise 4h Quadratic Expressions

1. Factorise:
   a. $x^2 + x - 12$
   b. $y^2 + 4y - 21$
   c. $x^2 + x - 20$
   d. $m^2 - 3m - 10$
   e. $x^2 - 6x + 8$
   f. $a^2 - 10a + 9$
   g. $x^2 + 11x - 12$
   h. $m^2 + m - 42$
   i. $x^2 + 4x - 32$

2. Factorise:
   a. $2x^2 + 5x + 3$
   b. $10y^2 + 17y + 3$
   c. $3a^2 - 11a + 6$
   d. $2x^2 - 9x + 4$
   e. $3x^2 - x - 10$
   f. $3y^2 - 4y - 4$
   g. $6x^2 - 17x + 5$
   h. $8x^2 - 6x - 9$
   i. $12m^2 + m - 6$

3. Factorise:
   a. $3 + 2x - x^2$
   b. $6 + 5x + x^2$
   c. $20 - 9y + y^2$
   d. $3 + x - 2x^2$
   e. $4 - 4a - 3a^2$
   f. $6 + 13m - 5m^2$
   g. $25 - 20x + 4x^2$
   h. $9 - 27x + 20x^2$
   i. $6 + 5x - 6x^2$

Exercise 4i Factorising Fully

1. Factorise completely:
   a. $3x^2 - 3$
   b. $4y^2 - 36$
   c. $8a^2 - 2b^2$
   d. $18x^2 - 32y^2$
   e. $108x^2 - 12y^2$
   f. $5m^2 - 125n^2$
   g. $54a^2 - 6b^2$
   h. $18x^2 - 98$
   i. $320x^2 - 180y^2$

2. Factorise completely:
   a. $3x^2 + 3x - 6$
   b. $4x^2 - 4x - 8$
   c. $5x^2 - 10x - 75$
   d. $2a^2 + 2a - 40$
   e. $3m^2 - 21m + 30$
   f. $7x^2 - 35x + 42$
   g. $20x^2 + 10x - 10$
   h. $11x^2 - 11x - 66$
   i. $12x^2 - 12x - 9$

3. Factorise completely:
   a. $x^4 + x^2 - 6$
   b. $2a^4 - 7a^2 + 3$
   c. $2y^4 + 3y^2 - 5$

See pages 12–17 of Leckie & Leckie's Intermediate 2 Maths Revision Notes

5 Circles

UNIT 1

5.1 Exercise 5a Finding Arcs and Sectors

1. Each of these sectors of a circle, centre C, has radius as shown.
   Taking π = 3·14 calculate the length of arc AB. Do not use a calculator.

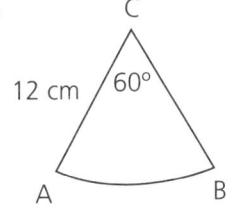

   a 5 cm, 72°

   b 12 cm, 60°

   c 6 cm, 120°

   d 40 cm, right angle at C

   e 40 cm, 144°

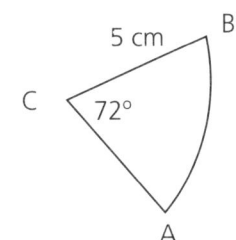

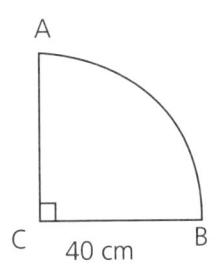

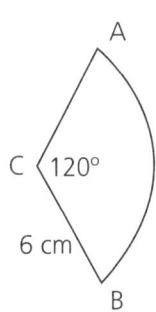

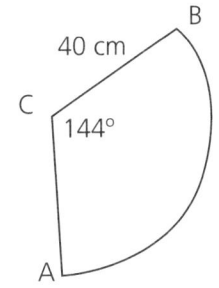

2. For each sector find its **i** perimeter **ii** area. Give your answers to three significant figures.

   a 4·8 cm, 115°

   b 12·4 cm, 32°

   c 18 cm, 244°

   d 3·2 m, 335°

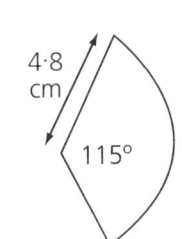

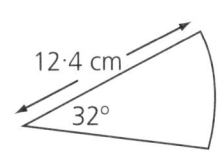

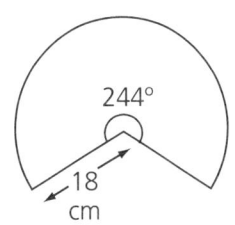

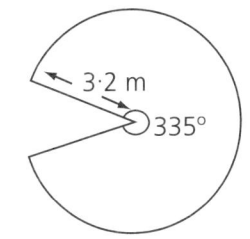

3. **a**

   i The minute hand is 8 cm long. How far does the tip of the hand travel in 25 minutes? 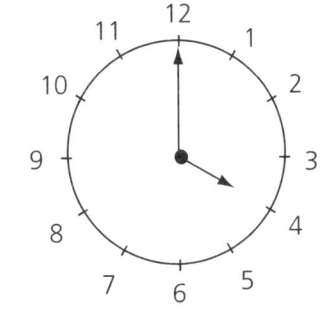

   ii The hour hand is 5 cm long. How far does its tip travel in $1\frac{1}{2}$ hours?

   (Give your answers to three significant figures.)

See Answers on pages 3–4 of answer booklet

19

5 Circles

b A regular pentagon PQRST is drawn in a circle, centre O, with radius 8 cm. Calculate, to two significant figures, the length of the arc PR.

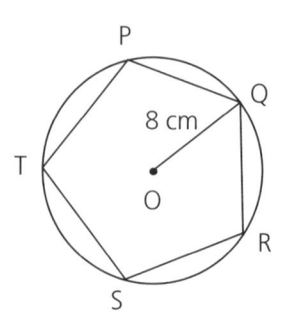

c This 1 metre pendulum swings through an arc of 38°. How far has tip A travelled for it to return to its starting position?

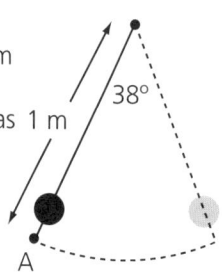

d AC and BD are arcs of circles with centres at O. OA is 12 cm and OB is 15 cm. Calculate the shaded area correct to two significant figures.

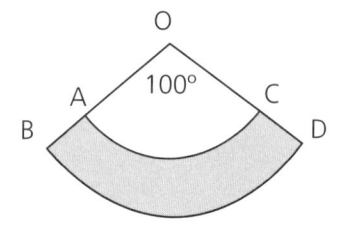

Exercise 5b Finding the angle at the Centre

1. For each sector ACB of a circle, calculate, to 1 decimal place, the size of angle ACB where C is the centre of the circle.

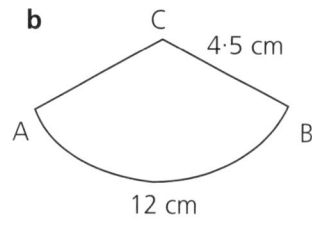

   a 5 cm, 12 cm

   b 4·5 cm, 12 cm

   c 3 cm, 13 cm

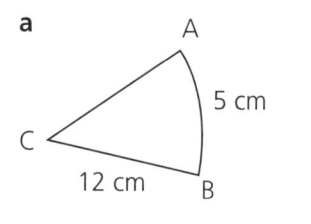

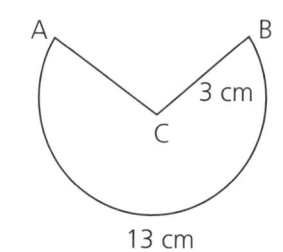

2. A pendulum tip travels along an arc AB of a circle. The arc is 12 cm. If the pendulum has length 30 cm, through what size of angle does it swing from A to B. Give your answer to 1 decimal place.

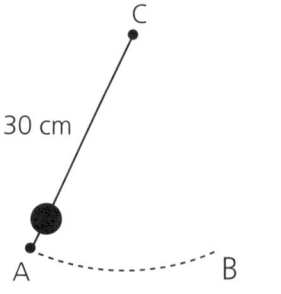

Exercise 5c Tangent Properties

For each Circle/Tangent diagram, find the value of x giving your answers to three significant figures where necessary.

1. x cm, 6 cm, 8 cm

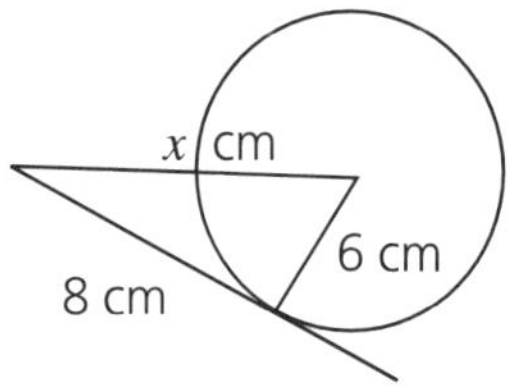

2. x cm, 11 cm, 13 cm

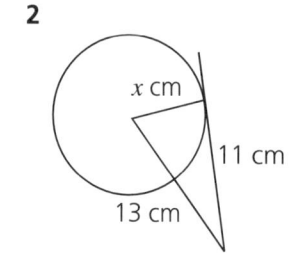

3. x cm, 9·5 cm, 21·5 cm

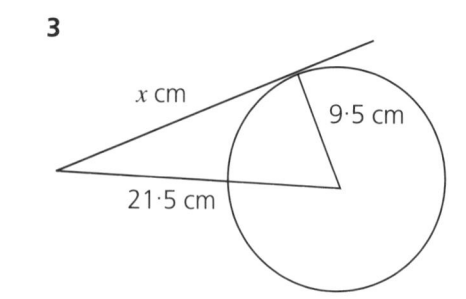

See pages 17–20 of Leckie & Leckie's Intermediate 2 Maths Revision Notes

5 Circles

UNIT 1

5.5 Exercise 5d Angles in a Semicircle

1 In each diagram DC is a tangent to the circle with centre O and point of contact C. Show all working.

a Calculate the size of angle BAC.

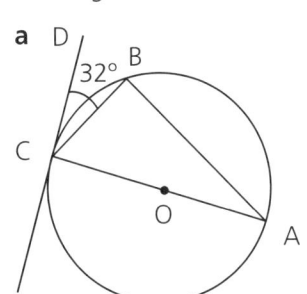

b Calculate the size of angle BCD.

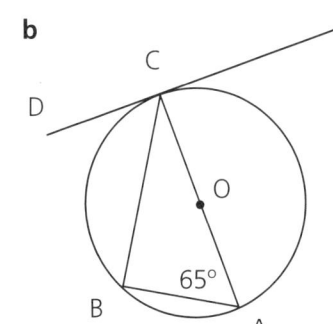

c OD and BC are parallel. Calculate the size of angle ODC.

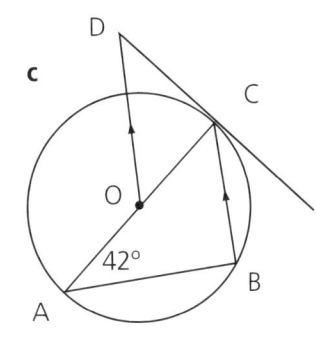

d OD and BC are parallel. Calculate the size of angle BAC.

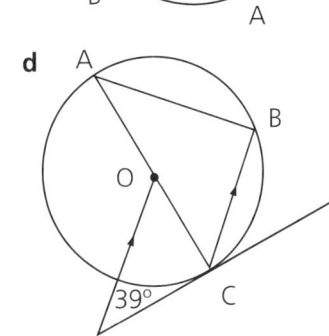

e Calculate the size of angle BAF.

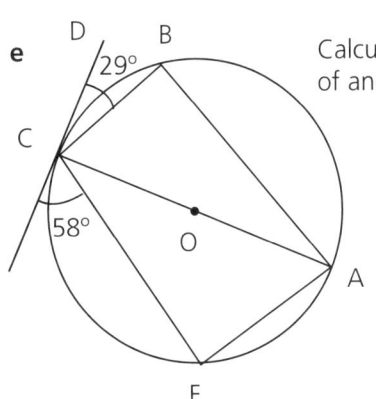

f Calculate the size of angle BCF.

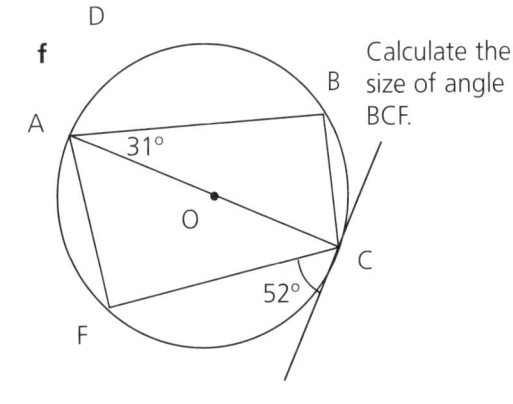

2 In each of these semicircle diagrams calculate x correct to three significant figures:

a 7·4 cm, 3·2 cm, x cm

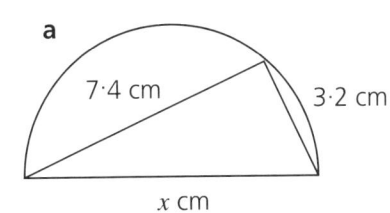

b 2·5 cm, 3 cm, x cm

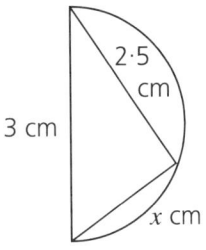

c 4·2 m, x m, 3·2 m

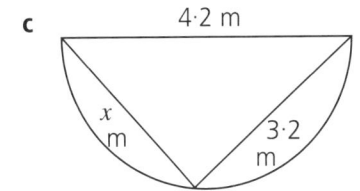

5.6 Exercise 5e Symmetry and Chords

1 a TU is a tangent to the circle, centre O. Calculate the size of angle TOS.

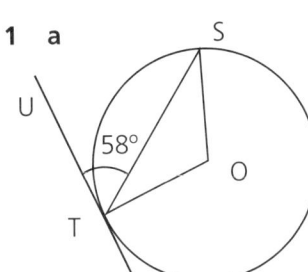

b CD is a tangent to the circle, centre O. Calculate the size of angle OBC.

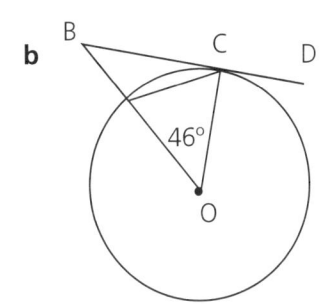

See Answers on page 4 of answer booklet

21

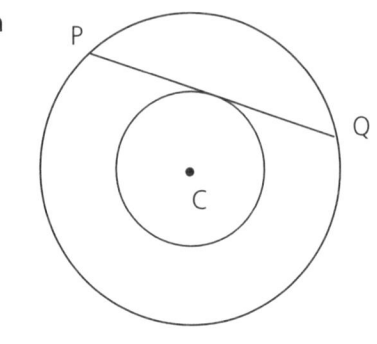

5 Circles

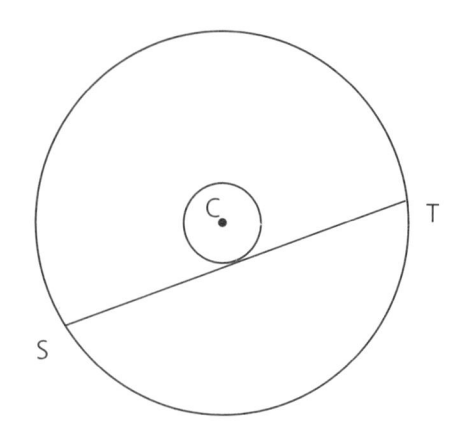

2 a C is the centre of two concentric circles. PQ is a tangent of the smaller circle and a chord of the larger circle. PQ is 24 cm and the radius of the small circle is 9 cm. Calculate the radius of the large circle.

b C is the centre of two concentric circles. ST is a tangent to the smaller circle and a chord of the larger circle. ST is 24 cm and the radius of the large circle is 13 cm. Calculate the radius of the small circle.

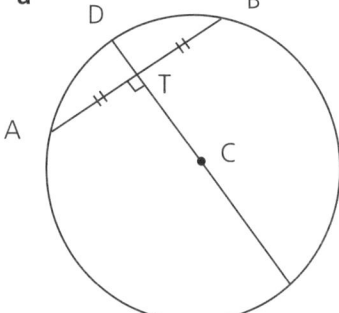

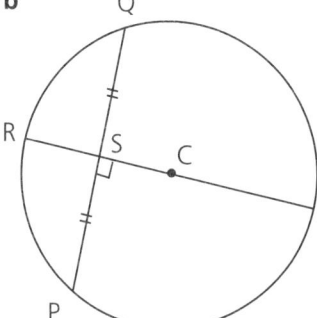

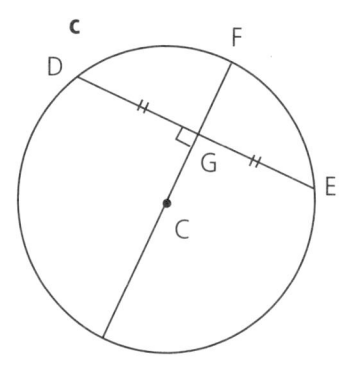

3 a Chord AB is 12 cm. Radius is 10 cm. Calculate the length of DT.

b Chord PQ is 10 m. Radius is 6 m. Calculate the length of RS.

c Chord DE is 26·8 cm. Radius is 16·4 cm. Calculate the length of FG.

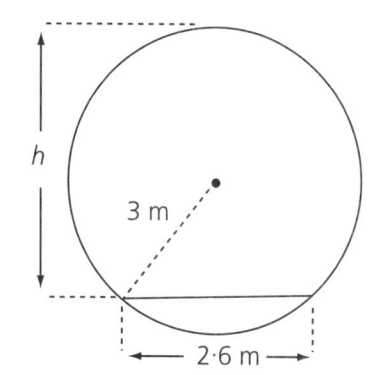

4 a This circular railway tunnel has radius 3 m. The width of the rail bed is 2·6 m. Calculate h, the height of the tunnel. Give your answer correct to two significant figures.

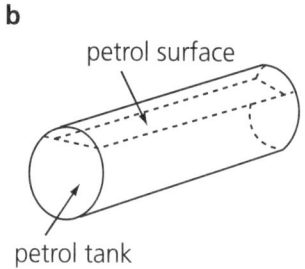

b This cross-section of a circular petrol tank with radius 2·2 m shows that the width of the petrol is 2·8 m at the top of the tank. Calculate d, the maximum depth of the petrol in the tank.

5

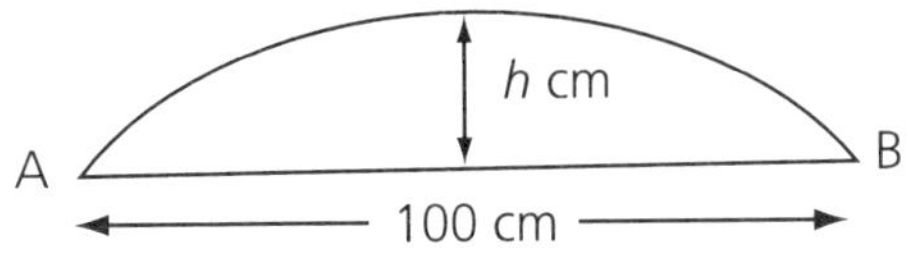

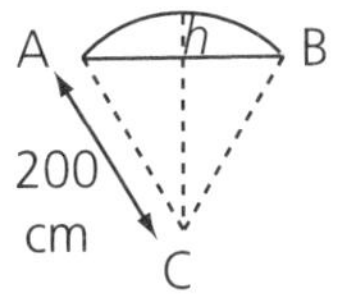

The diagram above shows a 'road hump' used for traffic calming. The curved part is formed from the arc of a circle.

In the diagram above and to the right:

C represents the centre of the circle

AB represents the horizontal surface of the road and is 100 cm

CA and CB are radii and are 200 cm each

Calculate the height, h cm, of the hump above the road. Give your answer correct to two significant figures.

See Answers on page 4 of answer booklet

6 Trigonometry

Exercise 6a Finding Sides and Angles

1 For each triangle calculate x correct to three significant figures:

a) 12 cm, 32°, x cm

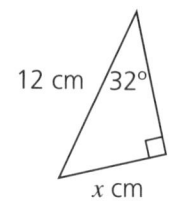

b) x cm, 73°, 15 cm

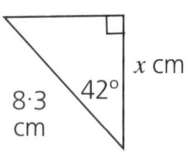

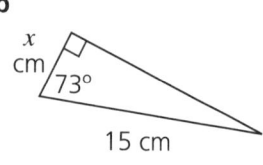

c) 31°, 5·1 cm, x cm

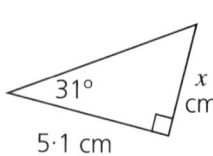

d) 8·3 cm, 42°, x cm

e) x cm, 73°, 23·5 cm

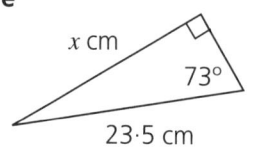

f) x cm, 53°, 2·9 cm

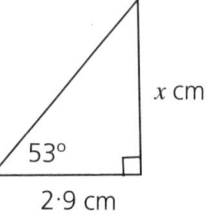

g) 25°, 3·5 cm, x cm

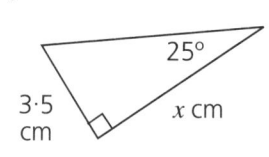

h) 10·8 cm, 46°, x cm

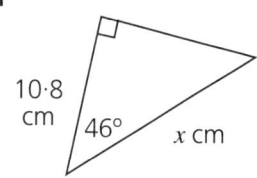

i) 0·5 m, 34°, x m

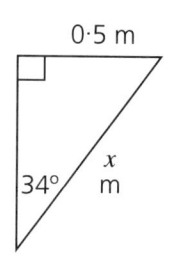

j) x mm, 68°, 36 mm

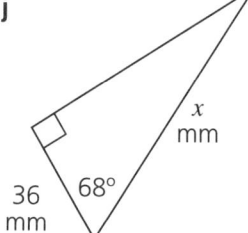

k) 1·3 m, 58°, x cm

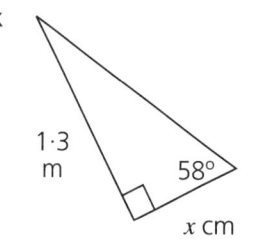

l) x km, 63°, 1·78 km

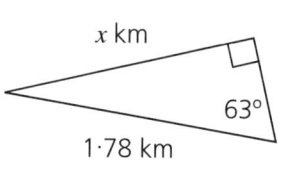

2 For each triangle calculate x correct to 1 decimal place:

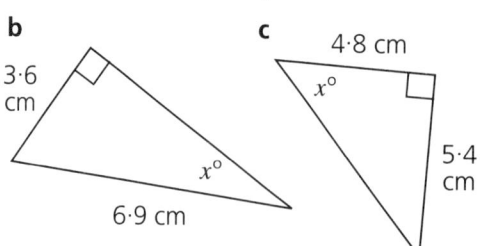

a) 9·2 cm, 6 cm, $x°$

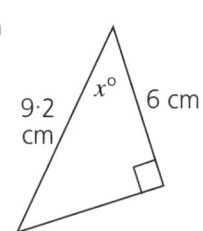

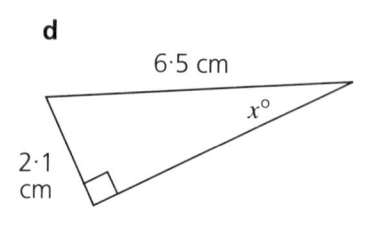

b) 3·6 cm, 6·9 cm, $x°$

c) 4·8 cm, 5·4 cm, $x°$

d) 6·5 cm, 2·1 cm, $x°$

e) 6·3 cm, 8·7 cm, $x°$

f) 3·1 cm, 6·4 cm, $x°$

g) 12·3 cm, 15·7 cm, $x°$

h) 30·8 cm, 27·5 cm, $x°$

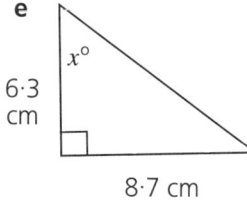

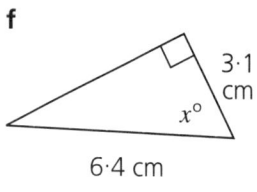

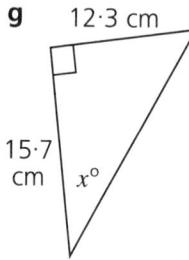

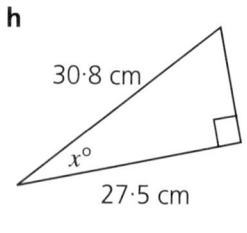

See pages 21–24 of Leckie & Leckie's Intermediate 2 Maths Revision Notes

6 Trigonometry

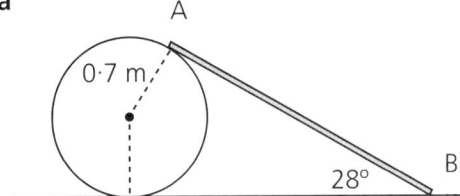

UNIT 2

3 a A metal rod AB is resting on a circular barrel with radius 0·7 m as shown. The rod is a tangent to the circle. If the rod makes an angle of 28° with the ground, calculate, to 2 significant figures, the length of the rod.

b This circular wheel has three evenly-spaced spokes OA, OB and OC as shown. The distance between the end of each pair of spokes is 15 cm. Calculate, to three significant figures, the length of each spoke.

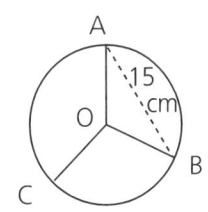

Exercise 6b Three-figure bearings

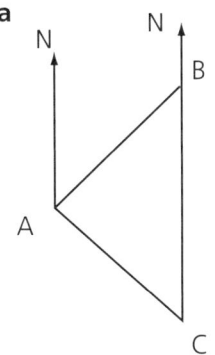

1 a From A, the bearing of B is 032° and the bearing of C is 118°. C is due south of B. Find the sizes of the angles of triangle ABC.

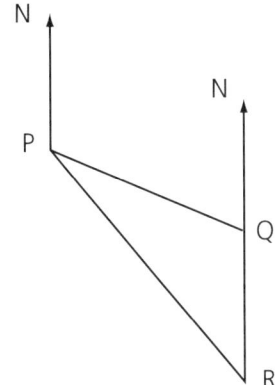

b From P, the bearing of Q is 115° and of R is 142°. R is due south of Q. Find the sizes of the angles in triangle PQR.

2 For each situation

  i   draw a diagram to illustrate the information

  ii find the sizes of the three angles of triangle ABC

  a From A, B is on a bearing of 152° and C is on a bearing of 195°. Also from C, B is on a bearing of 090° (i.e. it is due East of C).

  b B is due West of A. C is on a bearing of 190° from A and C is on a bearing of 130° from B.

  c From C, the bearing of A is 080°, B is due South of A. B is on a bearing of 130° from C.

See Answers on pages 4–5 of answer booklet

UNIT 2

6 Trigonometry

Exercise 6c   Area of a Triangle

1 Find the area of each triangle. Give your answers to three significant figures:

a 22 cm, 25 cm, 64°

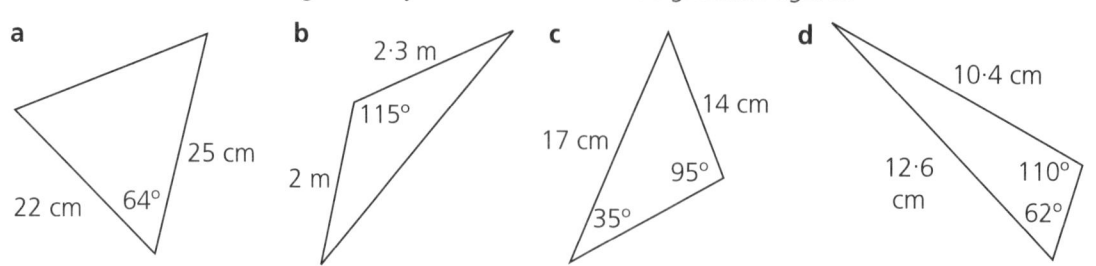

b 2·3 m, 2 m, 115°

c 14 cm, 17 cm, 95°, 35°

d 10·4 cm, 12·6 cm, 110°, 62°

2 Calculate the area of each of these regular polygons:

a ABC is an equilateral triangle drawn in a circle with radius OA of 12 cm.

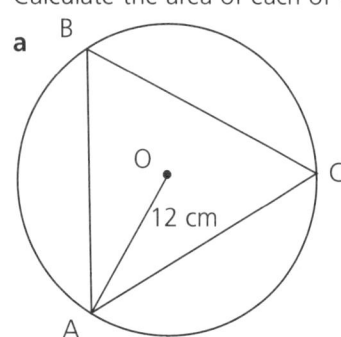

b ABCDEF is a regular hexagon drawn in a circle with radius OA of 8 cm.

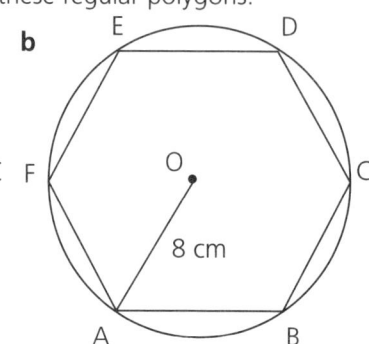

c ABCDE is a regular pentagon drawn in a circle with radius OA of 15 cm.

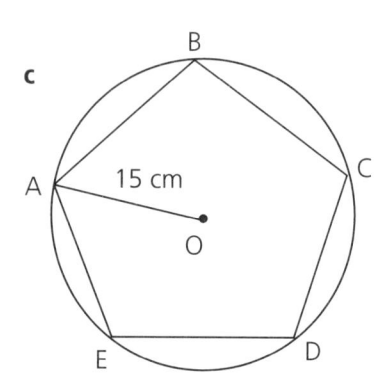

3 Calculate the area of each of these parallelograms:

a 7 cm, 65°, 12·6 cm

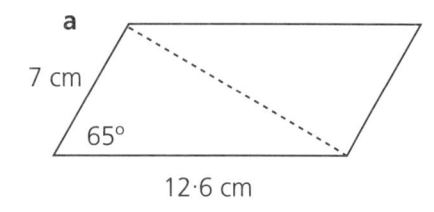

b 1·2 m, 115°, 3 m

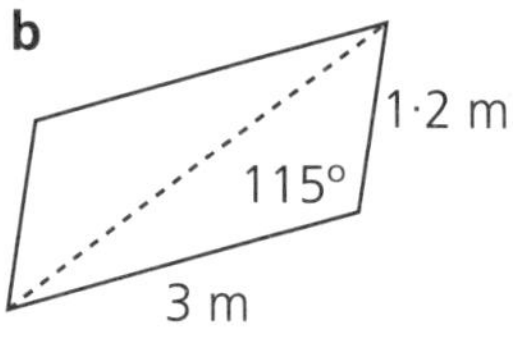

c 3·6 cm, 59°, 4·9 cm

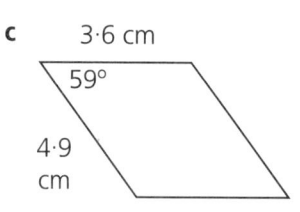

Exercise 6d The Sine Rule

1 a Find PQ. (P = 72°, R = 65°, QR = 9 cm)

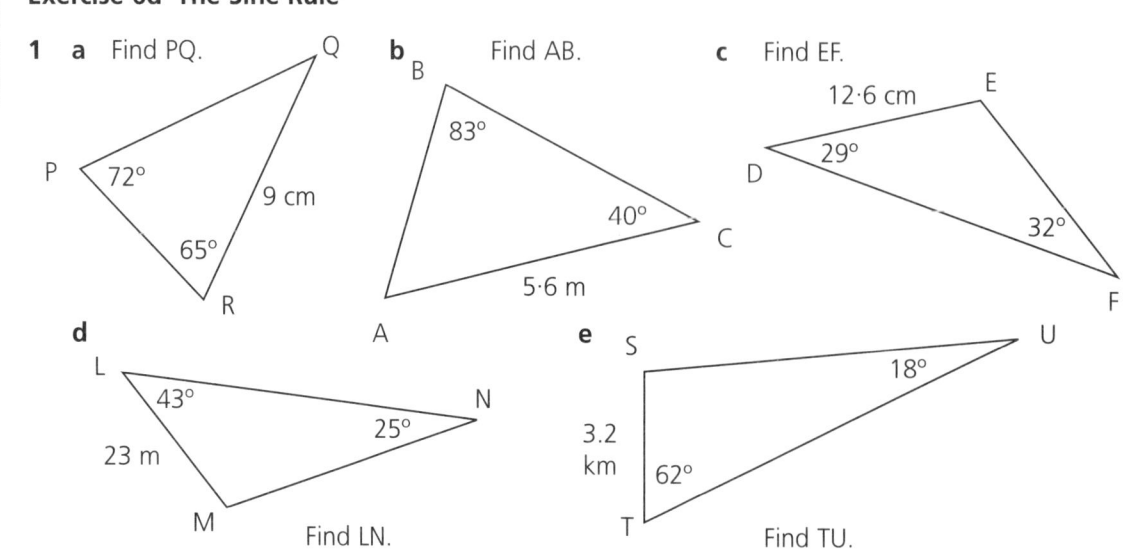

b Find AB. (B = 83°, C = 40°, AC = 5·6 m)

c Find EF. (DE = 12·6 cm, D = 29°, F = 32°)

d Find LN. (L = 43°, N = 25°, LM = 23 m)

e Find TU. (SU with 18° at U, ST = 3·2 km, T = 62°)

See pages 21–24 of Leckie & Leckie's Intermediate 2 Maths Revision Notes

6 Trigonometry

UNIT 2

f Triangle ABC with AB = 12 cm, BC = 13 cm, angle C = 29°.
Calculate angle BAC.

g Triangle JKL with angle J = 46°, JL = 2·6 m, KL = 2·3 m.
Calculate angle JKL.

h Triangle RST with RS side, ST = 58 cm, angle R = 106°, RT = 49 cm.
Calculate angle RST.

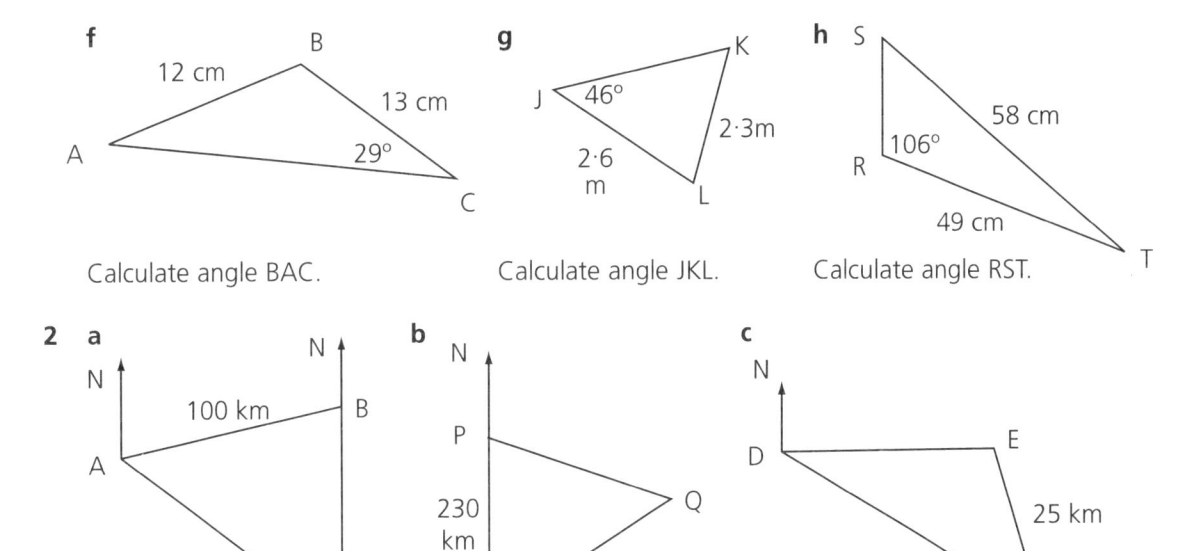

2 a From A, B is on a bearing of 080° and C is on a bearing of 125°, B is due North of C. AB = 100 km. Calculate AC to 3 significant figures.

b Q is on a bearing of 105° from P and 058° from R. R is due South of P. PR = 230 km. Calculate PQ to 2 significant figures.

c E is due East of D. F is on a bearing of 120° from D and 165° from E. EF = 25 km. Calculate DE to 2 significant figures.

3 a Two observers, 2·5 km apart, spot a helicopter (H). Observer A measures the angle of elevation of the helicopter as 25° and observer B measures it as 60°.
  i Calculate the distance of the helicopter from Observer B.
  ii Hence find the height of the helicopter above the ground.

b Boat P and boat Q are 100 m apart. From P, the angle of elevation of the top of a yacht's mast, T, is 042° and from Q it is 016°. Calculate the height of the top of the mast above sea-level. Give your answer to two significant figures.

c From Boat A the top of the lighthouse, T, has an angle of elevation of 18° and 32° from boat B. The two boats are 40 m apart.
  i Calculate length BT
  ii Hence calculate, to 2 significant figures, the height of the lighthouse.

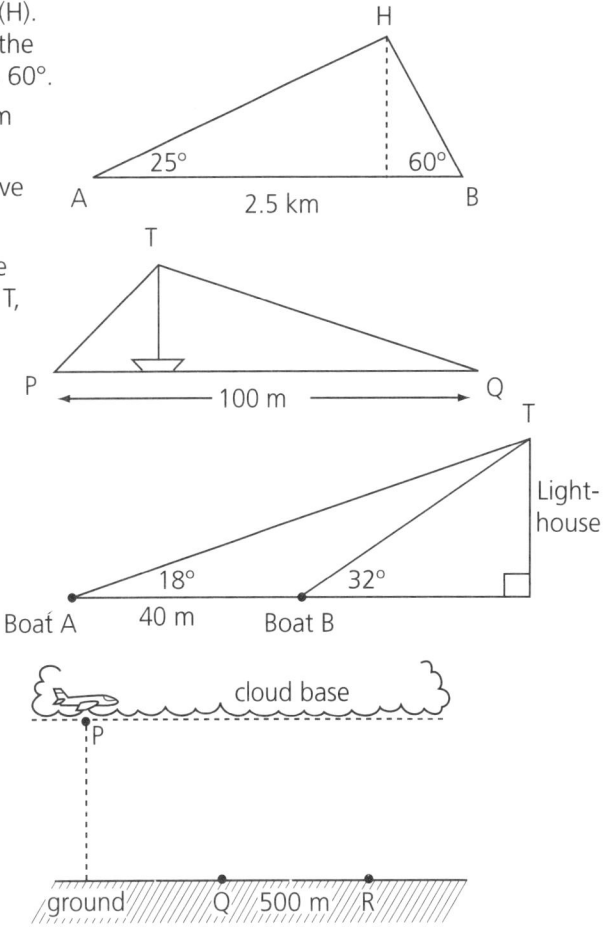

d Two observers Q and R are 500 m apart. A plane P is flying at the base of the clouds. From Q the angle of elevation of the plane is 43° and from R is 29°. Use this information to calculate the height of the clouds above the ground. (Answer to three significant figures.)

See Answers on page 5 of answer booklet

6 Trigonometry

Exercise 6e The Cosine Rule

1 a Triangle PQR with PQ = 6·2 cm, PR = 8·3 cm, angle P = 23°.
Calculate QR to two significant figures.

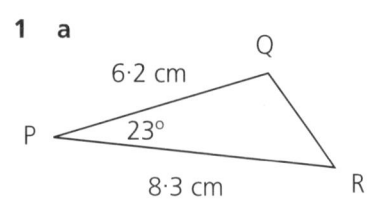

b Triangle ABC with AB = 13 m, AC = 9 m, angle A = 101°.
Calculate BC to three significant figures.

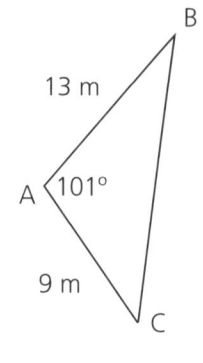

c Triangle STU with ST = 112 km, TU = 88 km, angle T = 25°.
Calculate SU to two significant figures.

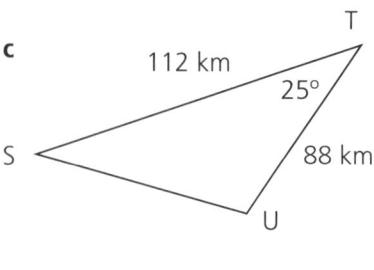

2 a Triangle PQR with PQ = 7 cm, QR = 6·7 cm, PR = 6 cm.
Calculate the size of angle QPR to one decimal place.

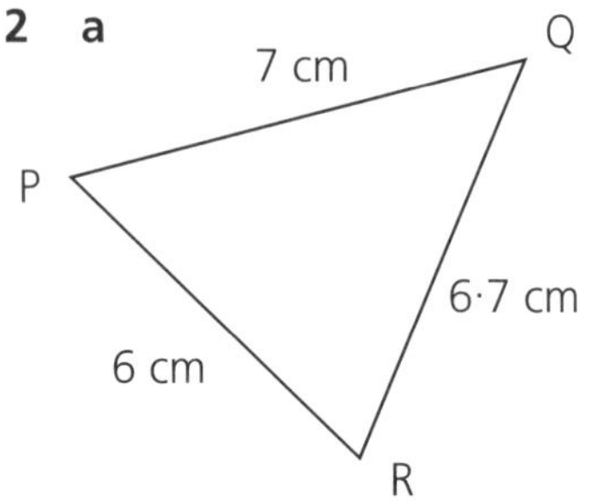

b Triangle ABC with AB = 14 cm, BC = 24·5 cm, AC = 30·2 cm.
Calculate the size of angle BAC to 1 decimal place.

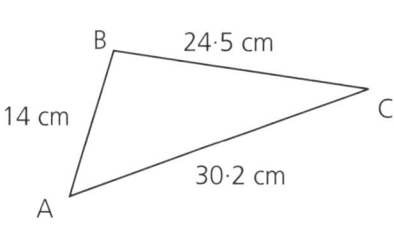

c Triangle STU with ST = 1·7 km, TU = 1·1 km, SU = 2·2 km.
Calculate the size of angle SUT to 1 decimal place.

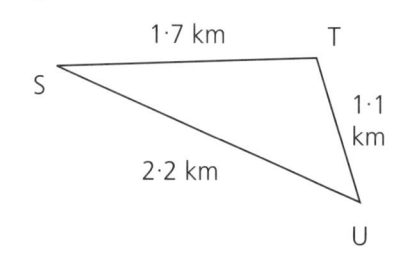

3 a Boat A is on a bearing of 035° and at a distance of 26 km from the harbour. Boat B is on a bearing of 075° and at a distance of 37 km from the harbour. Calculate the distance separating the two boats to the nearest km.

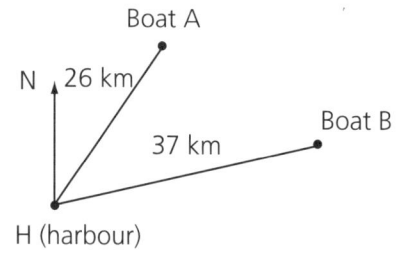

b From Boat P the bearing of boat Q is 050° and is at a distance of 800 metres. There is a rock R at a bearing of 062° from boat P and at a distance of 750 metres. Use this information to:
   i   draw a diagram to illustrate the situation
   ii write down the size of angle QPR
   iii calculate the distance, to the nearest metre, of the rock from boat Q.

7 Simultaneous linear equations

Exercise 7a Setting up a Linear Equation

1 Let £x be the cost of an adult's ticket and £y the cost of a child's ticket. Write down equations to represent these situations:

  a 5 adults and 4 children cost £31 in total

  b 12 adults and 2 children cost £64 in total

  c 3 adults with 15 children are charged £105 in total.

2 On a train journey, 1st class tickets cost £25 and 2nd class tickets cost £18. x 1st class tickets were sold and y 2nd class tickets were sold. Write down equations which represent:

  a the total number of tickets sold was 165

  b the total from sold tickets was £2250

  c the total number of tickets sold was 50

  d the total from ticket sales was £1005

3 Necklaces are made from large and small beads. The width of a large bead is x mm and the width of a small bead is y mm. Write down an equation to represent each necklace shown:

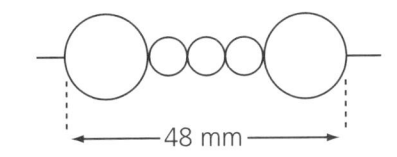

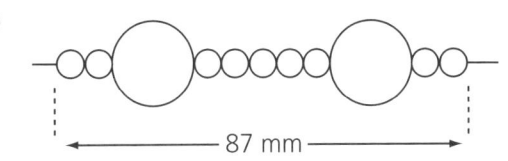

  a 48 mm

  b 87 mm

Exercise 7b Solving Problems Graphically

1 For each pair of equations, draw the two straight-line graphs and give the coordinates of the point of intersection of the lines.

  a $y = x + 1$ and $y = -x + 7$

  b $y = -2x + 7$ and $y = \frac{1}{2}x + 2$

  c $y = -2x + 6$ and $y = -\frac{1}{2}x$

2 A railway line on a map diagram is represented by the graph with equation $2y + x = 10$.
A motorway is represented on the same diagram by the graph with equation $y = \frac{1}{2}x + 2$. There is a station at the intersection of the railway line and the motorway.

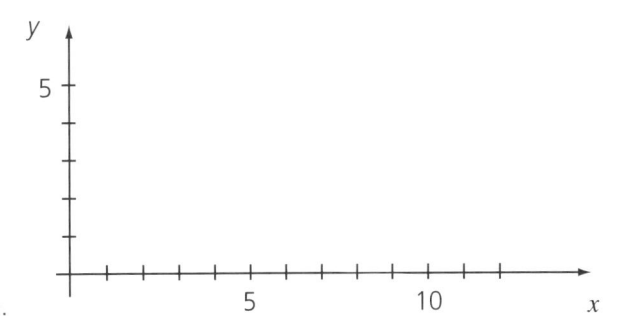

  a Draw the railway line on the diagram.

  b Draw the motorway on the diagram.

  c Write down the coordinates of the station.

UNIT 2

7 Simultaneous linear equations

Exercise 7c Solving Problems Algebraically

1. Solve algebraically these systems of equations:

   a $13x - 4y = 14$
      $5x + 2y = 16$

   b $3x - 5y = 8$
      $2x - 4y = 4$

   c $2x + y = 9$
      $5x + 3y = 23$

   d $3x + 5y = 7$
      $2x + 3y = 4$

   e $8x + 3y = 4$
      $3x - 2y = -11$

   f $5x - 2y = 19$
      $3x + 7y = -5$

2. a Iain bought 5 blank DVDs and 3 blank CDs for £5·80. Let x be the cost of a blank DVD and £y be the cost of a blank CD. Write down an equation in x and y which satisfies this information.

   b Kim, at the same shop, bought 4 blank DVDs and 2 blank CDs for £4·40. Write down a second equation in x and y which satisfies this information.

   c Find the cost of a blank DVD and the cost of a blank CD.

3. The circus is in town. Adult tickets cost £x and a child's ticket costs £y.

   a The Wilsons buy 4 adult tickets and 3 child tickets for £69. Write down an equation in x and y which satisfies this information.

   b The Simpsons buy 3 adult tickets and 2 child tickets for £50. Write down a second equation in x and y which satisfies this further information.

   c Find the cost of an adult ticket and the cost of a child's ticket.

4. Petrol costs £1·10 per litre for 'regular' and £1·30 per litre for 'super'.

   a The garage sold x litres of 'regular' and y litres of 'super' in the first hour of business, taking a total of £153. Write down an equation in x and y which satisfies the above condition.

   b A total of 130 litres were sold in this first hour. Write down a second equation in x and y which satisfies this further condition.

   c How many litres of each type were sold in the first hour?

8 Graphs, charts and tables

Exercise 8a Piecharts

Draw a piechart to illustrate the results of these surveys.

1

Favourite colour	Frequency
Black	2
Red	12
Yellow	2
Green	4

2

Favourite flavour	Frequency
Salt & vinegar	21
Bacon	11
Plain	9
Cheese & onion	19

3

Travel to school	Frequency
Bus	25
Walking	74
Car	49
Bike	32

4

Type of home	Frequency
Flat	16
Semi-detached	43
Detached	18
Terraced	13

Exercise 8b Cumulative Frequency

For each of these data sets construct a frequency table and add a cumulative frequency column.

1 In a class test the following marks were recorded:

5 4 7 8 9 1 6 10 8 10 8 5 5 9 6 4 9 4 10 7 5
9 5 2 7

2 The times taken by students to type a passage were (in minutes):

5 4 5 7 5 8 11 7 11 9 7 4 10 6 6

3 The hourly pay (£) for a group of students in holiday jobs were:

6 7 8 12 6 10 10 6 9 6 10 10 6 15 10 8 6 7 7 10

8 Graphs, charts and tables

Exercise 8c Dot Plots

1 The ages of twenty people attending a music concert were recorded:

17 17 19 18 20 14 21 18 19 16
19 17 18 15 20 18 16 20 17 18

   a Construct a dot plot for the data.
   b Describe the shape of the distribution.
   c What would you expect the 'average age of the concert-goer' to be?

2 The cost, to the nearest penny, of a litre of petrol at 25 petrol stations was recorded:

98 100 99 100 99 101 102 99 97 107 98 103 102
101 99 100 100 97 104 99 106 99 100 99 98

   a Construct a dot plot for the data.
   b Describe the shape of the distribution.
   c What would you expect the 'average cost per litre' to be?

3 The number of visitors each day to a local museum was recorded during the course of a month:

12 15 15 11 16 14 17 18 20 21 14 10 17 22 19
17 18 17 13 18 15 15 16 10 19 13 16 15 16 16

   a Construct a dot plot for the data.
   b Describe the shape of the distribution.
   c What would you expect the 'average number of visitors per day' to be?

Exercise 8d Quartiles

For the following sets of data find:

   a the median   **b** the lower quartile   **c** the upper quartile

1 8 4 5 8 4 7 4 5 6 9 3

2 3·5 3·1 3·2 3·6 3·0 3·1

3 16 12 19 15 17 14 20 17 14

4 77 85 77 81 74 86 80 80 76 79 76 87

5 0·9 1·4 0·6 1·6 1·7 0·8 1·4 0·6 1·1 1·0

See pages 28–31 of Leckie & Leckie's Intermediate 2 Maths Revision Notes

8 Graphs, charts and tables

UNIT 2

6
```
2 | 5 7 8
3 | 8 9
4 | 0 0 5 6 7 9
5 | 1 3 3 4 8
6 | 3 5 7 9
7 | 0
```
n = 21   3|8 represents 38

7
```
0 | 8 9 9
1 | 0 0 3 4 7 7 8
2 | 0 2 2 3 5 6
3 | 1 2
4 |
5 | 4 7
```
n = 20   0|8 represents 0·8

8

```
                •
                •        •
        •   •   •   •
    •   •   •   •   •   •
•   •   •   •   •   •   •
────┼───┼───┼───┼───┼───┼───┼───
   23  24  25  26  27  28  29
```

9

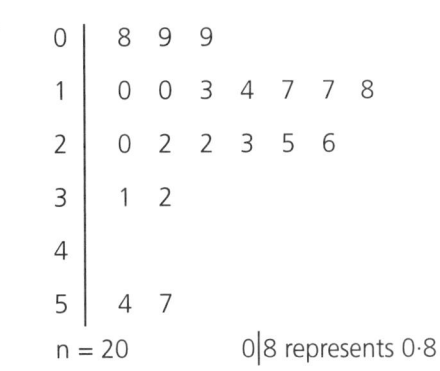

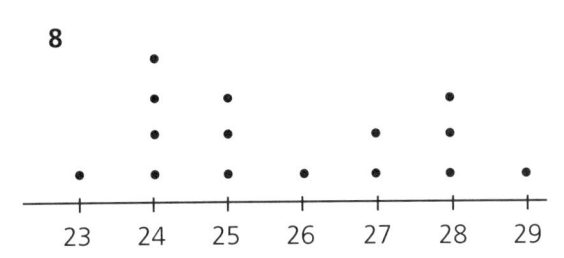

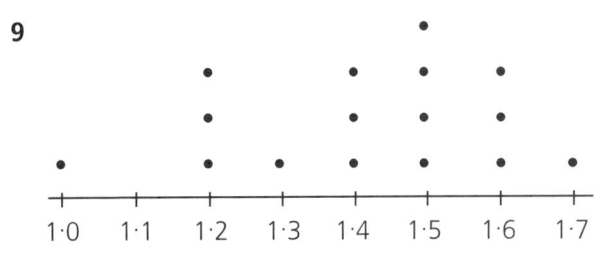

```
                                •
                        •   •       •
                •       •   •       •
•               •   •   •   •   •   •
┼───┼───┼───┼───┼───┼───┼───┼
1·0  1·1  1·2  1·3  1·4  1·5  1·6  1·7
```

8.6 **Exercise 8e Boxplots**

1 Draw a boxplot for each dataset in Exercise 8d.

2 Tubes of 'sugardrop' sweets contain 'on average 100 sweets per tube' claim the manufacturers. A sample of fifteen tubes contain the following numbers of sweets:

97   98   102   97   100   98   101   101   100   100   102   95   100   96   97

  a Find the median, lower quartile and upper quartile from this data.

  b Comment on the manufacturers' claim.

  c Construct a boxplot for this data.

  d Another sample gave the following boxplot.

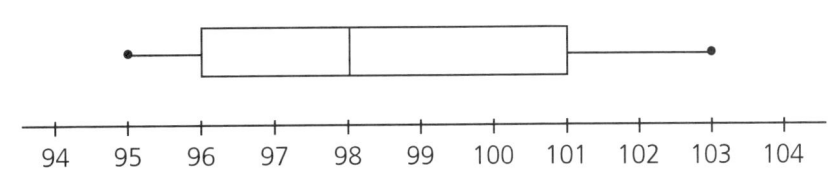

```
        94  95  96  97  98  99  100  101  102  103  104
```

Does this new data support the manufacturers' claim? Give a reason for your answer.

See Answers on page 7 of answer booklet

8 Graphs, charts and tables

3 A class of 25 students was asked how many hours they spend watching television each week. The results are shown:

5 14 17 2 16 8 9 14 7 4 11 2 10
8 12 3 13 5 5 15 2 3 16 4 9

a Find the median, lower quartile and upper quartile from this data.

b Construct a boxplot for this data.

c The same class of students was asked how many hours they spent on their computer during the course of a week. Here is the boxplot for this data.

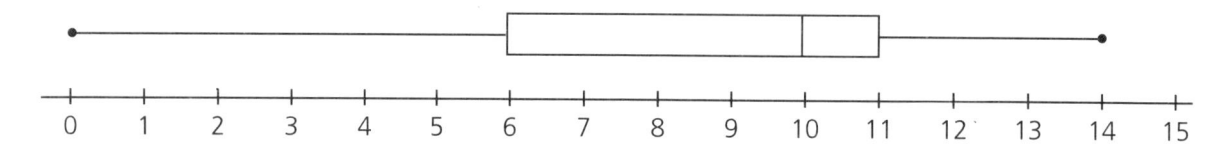

Compare the two boxplots and comment.

4 A school recorded the number of absentees on eighteen Mondays during the course of a term. The results are shown in this stem and leaf diagram:

```
1 | 0 2 3 3 4 5
2 | 4 6 7 9
3 | 0 5 8
4 | 1 2 4 6
5 | 4
```

n = 18   1|0 represents 10 absentees

a Use this data to find the median, lower quartile and upper quartile.

b Draw a boxplot to illustrate this data.

c During the course of the same term absentees on the eighteen Fridays were also recorded. Here is the boxplot illustrating the data for Friday absentees:

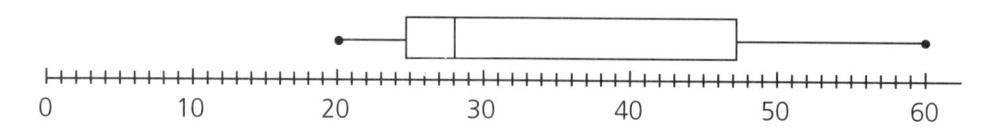

By comparing the two boxplots, make two appropriate comments about the number of absentees that term on Mondays and Fridays.

9 Statistics UNIT 2

Exercise 9a Averages and Range

1 For each data set calculate:

  i the range

  ii the mean (to two significant figures where necessary)

  iii the median

  iv the mode

  a 5, 8, 2, 1, 3, 3, 7, 6, 5, 5

  b 23, 16, 17, 11, 22, 15, 13, 16, 23, 16, 20, 21

  c 3, 5, 4, $4\frac{1}{2}$, $3\frac{1}{2}$, $5\frac{1}{2}$, 5, $4\frac{1}{2}$, 5, 6, $3\frac{1}{2}$, 5, $4\frac{1}{2}$, $5\frac{1}{2}$, 3

2 Calculate:

  i the range

  ii the mean (to two significant figures where necessary)

  iii the median

  iv the mode

  for the data shown in the following frequency tables

  a

Family size	1	2	3	4	5	6
Frequency	4	12	7	4	2	1

  (The data shows the family size (no. of children) for each one of 30 pupils in a class.)

  b

No. of minutes	9	10	11	12	13	14	15
Frequency	15	12	8	7	5	2	1

  (The data shows the time taken by 50 workers to complete a task.)

Exercise 9b Quartiles and Semi-interquartile Range

1 For each data set calculate:

  i the median

  ii the lower and upper quartiles

  iii the semi-interquartile range

  a 1, 3, 4, 4, 5, 7, 7

  b 15, 13, 16, 19, 22, 12, 13, 16, 20, 18, 17, 25, 22

  c 3·7, 4·0, 3·3, 3·9, 4·4, 3·6, 4·3, 3·2, 3·7, 3·2

  d 93, 86, 107, 89, 93, 93, 82, 101, 88, 99, 85, 86

See Answers on pages 7–8 of answer booklet

UNIT 2

9 Statistics

2 A maths class consisted of 15 boys and 15 girls. In a class test the scores out of ten were as follows:

Girls: 5 8 6 8 4 4 6 7 9 8 5 7 0 8 7

Boys: 1 6 3 3 8 9 5 10 3 10 7 8 2 10 3

Calculate the median and semi-interquartile range for each of these data sets and comment on the results.

3 The time spent eating lunch was recorded for a random sample of 20 boys at a school. The stem and leaf diagram below shows the data:

Time (minutes) spent eating lunch

```
0 | 8 8 9 9
1 | 0 5 6 6 7 7 8 9 9
2 | 0 0 1 2 3 7
3 | 5
```

n = 20   1|5 represents 15 minutes

a For this data calculate:

  i   the median

  ii   the lower quartile

  iii the upper quartile

  iv   the semi-interquartile range

b A similar sample of 20 girls at the same school gave a median time of 16 minutes with a semi-interquartile range of $2\frac{1}{2}$. Compare these statistics with those obtained from the boys' data and comment on the results.

9.3 Exercise 9c Standard Deviation

1 For each data set calculate:

  i   the mean

  ii the standard deviation (using an appropriate formula) to two significant figures where necessary.

  a 12, 15, 17, 18, 13

  b 3·6, 2·8, 3·1, 3·2, 3·0, 2·9

2 A random sample of matchboxes is checked. The total numbers of matches in the boxes are:

61, 63, 60, 58, 63

  a Calculate the mean and the standard deviation (to two significant figures) for the sample using an appropriate formula.

  b 'On average 60 matches' Comment on this statement that is printed on each box.

See pages 32–36 of Leckie & Leckie's Intermediate 2 Maths Revision Notes

9 Statistics

3 Claire is comparing download prices, in pence, for music files. She visited six on-line music stores. Prices per track were:

63, 60, 57, 62, 65, 59

  a Find the mean price for a download.

  b Use an appropriate formula to calculate, to 1 decimal place, the standard deviation for this data set. Show clearly all your working.

  c Equivalent prices at retail shops have the same mean but with a standard deviation of 4·5. Make a valid comparison between the download cost and the retail shop cost per track.

4 Buying prices, in £, for lambs at a market town auction are:

124, 128, 121, 118, 145, 120, 125, 105, 117, 122.

This was a random sample of ten prices in June.

  a Calculate the mean price of a lamb.

  b Use an appropriate formula to calculate, to 1 decimal place, the standard deviation for this data set. Show clearly all your working.

  c Make two valid comparisons between these market town auction prices and a rural auction in June where the mean price was £119 with the standard deviation being 3·5.

5 The time, in minutes, taken to travel to school was recorded for a random sample of ten pupils:

2, 27, 5, 16, 11, 3, 19, 23, 31, 8.

For this data $\Sigma x = 145$ and $\Sigma x^2 = 3059$ where x is the time, in minutes, taken to travel to school by the pupils.

  a Calculate the mean time taken to travel to school.

  b Using an appropriate formula, calculate the standard deviation.

  c For statistical purposes 1 minute was added to each time. Calculate the new mean time and standard deviation.

6 The heights, in millimetres, of 12 seedlings are recorded:

14, 15, 30, 24, 26, 21, 18, 23, 22, 23, 29, 19.

For this data $\Sigma x = 264$ and $\Sigma x^2 = 6082$ where x is the height in millimetres.

  a Calculate the mean height.

  b Using an appropriate formula, calculate the standard deviation for these heights.

  c Two days later each seedling had grown exactly 2 millimetres. State:

  i the mean

  ii the standard deviation of the new heights.

9 Statistics

9.4

Exercise 9d Scattergraphs and Lines of Best Fit

1. A scattergraph is shown comparing the Maths score, m%, with the French score, f%, gained by a class of 21 pupils at a particular school. Pupil A scored 0% in Maths and 84% in French. Pupil B scored 80% in Maths and 52% in French.

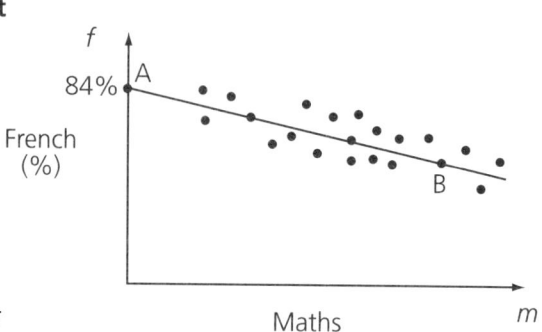

   a Find the equation of the line of best fit AB.

   b Zoe scored 70% in Maths. Use your answer to part **a** to predict her French score.

2. A group of pupils were asked to memorise a string of numbers in a minute. A similar task was given with a string of random letters. The results are shown in the scattergraph. A line of best fit has been drawn.

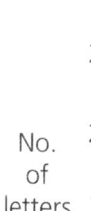

   a Find the equation of the line of best fit.

   b Use your answer to part **a** to predict the number of letters memorised by a pupil who can memorise 30 numbers.

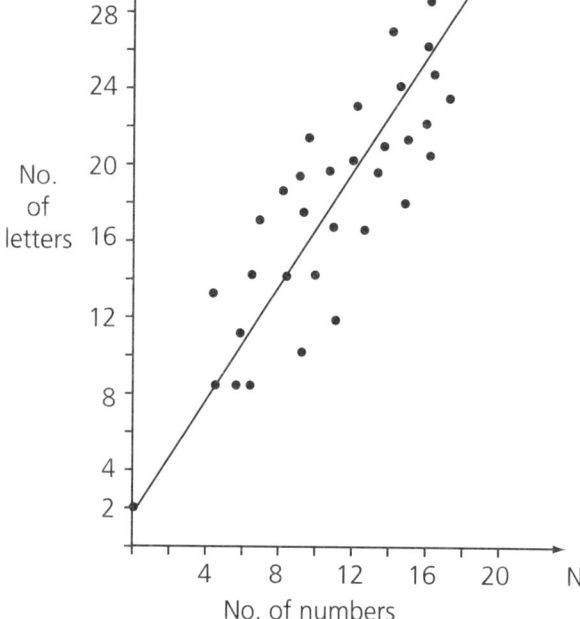

9.5

Exercise 9e Probability

1. The family size (number of children) for a group of pupils was recorded.

   1, 7, 4, 4, 3, 5, 8, 3, 3, 4

   What is the probability that a pupil chosen at random from this group has family size:

   a equal to 4   b less than 4   c greater than 7

   d less than 9   e greater than 8   f between 2 and 6?

See pages 32–36 of Leckie & Leckie's Intermediate 2 Maths Revision Notes

9 Statistics

UNIT 2

2 This stem and leaf diagram shows the heights of a group of pupils.

```
11 | 8  8  9
12 | 0  0  4  7  8  8
13 | 4  5  5  6  7  7  7  9
14 | 0  0  2
```

n = 20   11|8 represents 118 centimetres

What is the probability that a pupil chosen at random from this group has height

- **a** 120 cm
- **b** greater than 139 cm
- **c** less than 140 cm
- **d** between 125 cm and 138 cm?

3 The table shows the possible outcomes when the die is rolled and the spinner spun:

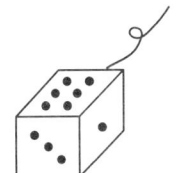

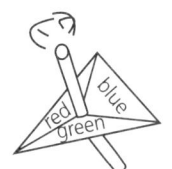

	1	2	3	4	5	6
Red	R, 1					
Blue			B, 3			
Green						G, 6

- **a** Copy and complete the table
- **b** What is the probability that the outcome is:
  - **i** blue with an odd number
  - **ii** not green with a number less than 3
  - **iii** red or green with a 4 or 5
  - **iv** red with a factor of 6?

10 Further algebraic operations

Exercise 10a Cancelling Fractions

1 a Factorise
   i $x^2 + x - 6$ ii $2x - 4$
   b Hence express $\dfrac{x^2 + x - 6}{2x - 4}$ in its simplest form.

2 a Factorise completely $4x^2 + 12x$ **b** Factorise $x^2 - 2x - 15$
   c Hence express $\dfrac{4x^2 + 12x}{x^2 - 2x - 15}$ in its simplest form.

3 Simplify:

a $\dfrac{y^2 + 4y}{y}$ b $\dfrac{a^2 - a - 6}{a^2 - 9}$ c $\dfrac{x^2 - 6x + 5}{x^2 + 5x - 6}$

d $\dfrac{(3x - 1)^2}{2(3x - 1)}$ e $\dfrac{(2x + 3)^2}{6x + 9}$ f $\dfrac{5x - 30}{x^2 - 12x + 36}$

g $\dfrac{3x - 3}{2x^2 - 4x + 2}$ h $\dfrac{4x^2 + 8x + 4}{2x^2 - 2}$ i $\dfrac{2a^2 - 18}{4a^2 - 24a + 36}$

j $\dfrac{m^2 - n^2}{m + n}$ k $\dfrac{2y^2 + 5y - 3}{2y^2 + 7y - 4}$ l $\dfrac{5x^2 - 20}{3x^2 - 5x - 2}$

Exercise 10b Multiplying Fractions

Express in simplest form:

1 $\dfrac{y}{8} \times \dfrac{4x}{y^2}$ 2 $\dfrac{ab}{2} \times \dfrac{4}{b^2}$ 3 $\dfrac{3x}{4} \times \dfrac{2y}{3x}$

4 $\dfrac{1}{2} \times \dfrac{8a}{ab}$ 5 $\dfrac{a^2}{b} \times \dfrac{b^2}{a}$ 6 $\dfrac{3ab}{4} \times \dfrac{4}{b}$

7 $\dfrac{2(x - 3)^2}{3} \times \dfrac{6}{x - 3}$ 8 $\dfrac{5}{4(2x - 1)^2} \times \dfrac{2(2x - 1)}{15}$ 9 $\dfrac{3ab}{4(a - b)} \times \dfrac{8(a - b)^2}{3a^2}$

Exercise 10c Dividing Fractions

Simplify:

1 $\dfrac{2a}{b} \div \dfrac{4}{b}$ 2 $\dfrac{x^2}{y} \div \dfrac{x}{2y}$ 3 $\dfrac{xy}{5} \div \dfrac{x^2}{10}$ 4 $\dfrac{3a^2}{b} \div \dfrac{a}{b^2}$

5 $\dfrac{3x^2}{4} \div \dfrac{3x}{2}$ 6 $\dfrac{2}{a + b} \div \dfrac{4}{a + b}$ 7 $\dfrac{x - y}{x + y} \div \dfrac{3}{x + y}$ 8 $\dfrac{4}{x + y} \div \dfrac{2}{(x + y)^2}$

See pages 37–42 of Leckie & Leckie's Intermediate 2 Maths Revision Notes

10 Further algebraic operations

Exercise 10d Adding and Subtracting Fractions

Express as a fraction in its simplest form:

1. $\dfrac{3}{x} + \dfrac{2}{x+2}$, $x \neq 0$, $x \neq -2$

2. $\dfrac{1}{x+1} + \dfrac{2}{x}$, $x \neq 0$, $x \neq -1$

3. $\dfrac{5}{x} - \dfrac{2}{x-3}$, $x \neq 0$, $x \neq 3$

4. $\dfrac{7}{x} - \dfrac{1}{x-2}$, $x \neq 0$, $x \neq 2$

5. $\dfrac{2}{a^2} - \dfrac{1}{a}$, $a \neq 0$

6. $\dfrac{1}{y} + \dfrac{5}{2y}$, $y \neq 0$

7. $\dfrac{4}{ab} - \dfrac{1}{a}$, $a \neq 0$, $b \neq 0$

8. $\dfrac{3}{x+1} + \dfrac{2}{x-1}$, $x \neq -1$, $x \neq 1$

Exercise 10e Changing the Subject of a Formula

Change the subject of the formula:

1. $a = \dfrac{bc}{R}$ to c

2. $\dfrac{M}{xy} = 5$ to M

3. $\dfrac{\pi r^2}{4} = 7$ to r

4. $P = x^2 - Q$ to x

5. $R = \dfrac{r^2 + 5}{2}$ to r

6. $K = \dfrac{x^2 - a}{b}$ to x

7. $A = x^2B - 2$ to x

8. $L + ax^2 = M$ to x

9. $4a - 5b = k$ to a

10. $m = 4x - 3y$ to x

11. $5n + 2 = 3m$ to n

12. $\dfrac{a - 2b}{c} = Q$ to a

13. $\dfrac{5m + 3n}{2} = k$ to m

14. $P = \dfrac{3a - 5b}{c}$ to a

15. $\dfrac{2k^2 + 4}{m} = n$ to k

Exercise 10f Simplifying Surds

1. Express as a surd in its simplest form:

    a. $\sqrt{20}$
    b. $\sqrt{32}$
    c. $\sqrt{63}$
    d. $\sqrt{44}$
    e. $\sqrt{242}$

2. Simplify:

    a. $5\sqrt{12}$
    b. $3\sqrt{50}$
    c. $4\sqrt{32}$
    d. $2\sqrt{72}$
    e. $7\sqrt{68}$

UNIT 3

10 Further algebraic operations

3 Simplify:

a $\sqrt{27} - \sqrt{12}$ b $\sqrt{45} - \sqrt{5}$ c $\sqrt{50} + \sqrt{98}$

d $\sqrt{75} - \sqrt{3} + \sqrt{48}$ e $\sqrt{28} - \sqrt{7} + \sqrt{63}$ f $\sqrt{54} - 2\sqrt{6} + \sqrt{150}$

g $\sqrt{75} - \sqrt{12} + \sqrt{300}$ h $\sqrt{45} + 2\sqrt{5} - \sqrt{20}$ i $\sqrt{28} + \sqrt{175} - 2\sqrt{7}$

10.9 Exercise 10g Rationalising the Denominator

Express as a fraction with a rational denominator giving your answer in simplest form:

1 $\dfrac{3}{\sqrt{2}}$ 2 $\dfrac{7}{\sqrt{3}}$ 3 $\dfrac{8}{\sqrt{2}}$ 4 $\dfrac{9}{\sqrt{3}}$

5 $\dfrac{16}{\sqrt{6}}$ 6 $\dfrac{6}{\sqrt{8}}$ 7 $\dfrac{5}{\sqrt{10}}$ 8 $\dfrac{1}{2\sqrt{2}}$

9 $\dfrac{2}{3\sqrt{5}}$ 10 $\dfrac{2}{3\sqrt{24}}$ 11 $\dfrac{\sqrt{30}}{\sqrt{3}}$ 12 $\dfrac{\sqrt{24}}{\sqrt{2}}$

13 $\dfrac{\sqrt{3}}{\sqrt{60}}$ 14 $\dfrac{3\sqrt{15}}{\sqrt{5}}$ 15 $\dfrac{2\sqrt{3}}{\sqrt{12}}$

10.10 Exercise 10h Working with Indices

1 Evaluate:

a $x^{\frac{3}{2}}$ when $x = 4$ b $y^{\frac{2}{3}}$ when $y = 27$ c $a^{\frac{1}{2}}$ when $a = 9$

d $x^{\frac{4}{3}}$ when $x = 8$ e $y^{-\frac{1}{2}}$ when $y = 25$ f $a^{-\frac{3}{2}}$ when $a = 16$

g $2x^{\frac{5}{2}}$ when $x = 4$ h $3y^{\frac{1}{3}}$ when $y = 8$

See pages 37–42 of Leckie & Leckie's Intermediate 2 Maths Revision Notes

10 Further algebraic operations

UNIT 3

2 Simplify:

   a $x^2(1 - x^{-2})$ **b** $3a^{-\frac{1}{2}} \times 2a^{\frac{3}{2}}$ **c** $8y^{\frac{5}{2}} \div 2y^{\frac{1}{2}}$

   d $\dfrac{2x^2 \times 3x}{x^3}$ **e** $\dfrac{a^{\frac{2}{3}} \times a^{\frac{1}{3}}}{a}$ **f** $x^{-2} \times (x^3)^2$

   g $\dfrac{a^{\frac{5}{2}}}{a^{\frac{3}{2}} \times a^{-1}}$ **h** $b^{-\frac{1}{2}}(2b^{\frac{3}{2}} + 3b^{\frac{1}{2}})$ **i** $\dfrac{3(a^{-2})^3 \times a^8}{a}$

   j $\dfrac{a^6 \times (a^2)^{-1}}{a^3}$ **k** $\dfrac{3x^{\frac{5}{2}} \times x^{-\frac{1}{2}}}{x}$ **l** $(c^3)^2 \times (c^{-2})^3$

   m $\sqrt{9x^6}$ **n** $\sqrt{4a^4} \times a^{-1}$ **o** $\dfrac{x^{\frac{1}{3}} \times x^{\frac{5}{3}}}{\sqrt{x^8}}$

3 Remove brackets and simplify:

   a $a^{-\frac{1}{2}}(a^{\frac{5}{2}} - 5a^{\frac{1}{2}})$ **b** $x^{\frac{1}{2}}\left(x^{\frac{3}{2}} + \dfrac{1}{x^{\frac{1}{2}}}\right)$ **c** $4y^{\frac{1}{2}}\left(y^{\frac{1}{2}} + \dfrac{1}{2}y^{-\frac{1}{2}}\right)$

   d $b^{-\frac{1}{2}}\left(b + \dfrac{1}{b^{\frac{1}{2}}}\right)$ **e** $5a^{-\frac{3}{2}}\left(a^2 - \dfrac{2}{5a^{\frac{1}{2}}}\right)$ **f** $2x^{-\frac{1}{2}}\left(\dfrac{1}{2}x^{\frac{1}{2}} + x^{-\frac{1}{2}}\right)$

11 Quadratic graphs and equations

Exercise 11a Quadratic Graphs

1. Each diagram shows the graph of $y = kx^2$. Find the value of k.

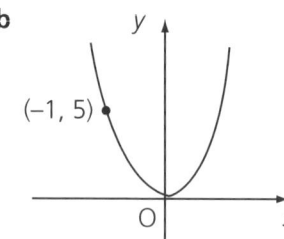

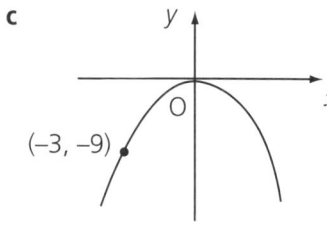

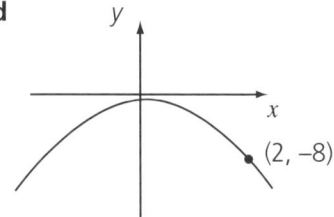

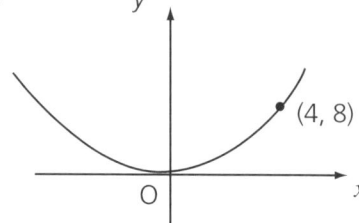

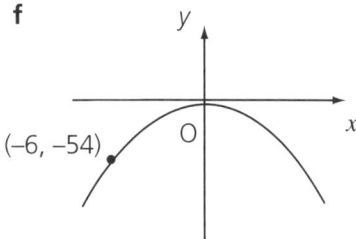

   a. (3, 27)

   b. (−1, 5)

   c. (−3, −9)

   d. (2, −8)

   e. (4, 8)

   f. (−6, −54)

   g. (−2, $^8/_3$)

   h. ($^1/_2$, $^3/_8$)

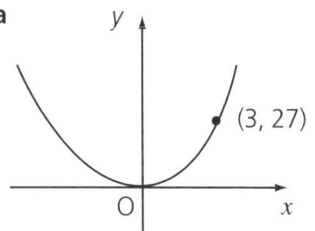

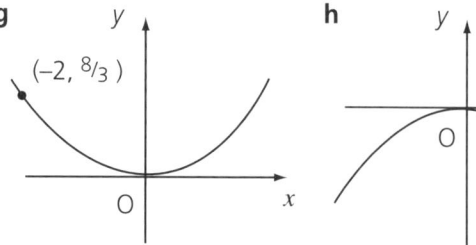

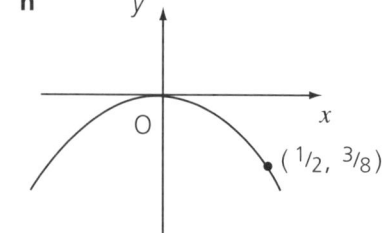

2. a. 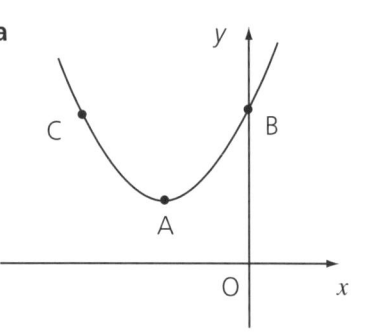 The diagram shows the graph of $y = (x + 3)^2 + 2$

   i State the coordinates of A, the minimum turning point.

   ii State the equation of the axis of symmetry.

   iii Find the coordinates of B, the y-axis intercept.

   iv B and C have the same y-coordinate. Find the coordinates of C.

   b. The diagram shows the graph of $y = (x − 5)^2 − 3$

   i State the coordinates of the minimum turning point.

   ii State the equation of the axis of symmetry.

   iii Find the coordinates of A, the y-axis intercept.

   iv Find the coordinates of B, the point on the curve with the same y-coordinate as point A.

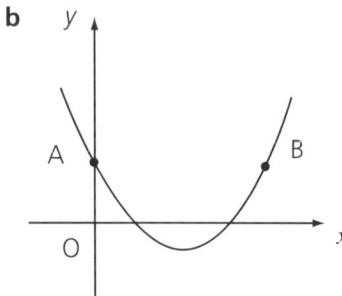

See pages 42–46 of Leckie & Leckie's Intermediate 2 Maths Revision Notes

11 Quadratic graphs and equations

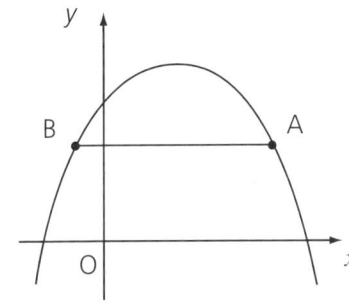

UNIT 3

c The diagram shows the graph of $y = 49 - (x - 4)^2$

  i State the coordinates of the maximum turning point.

  ii State the equation of the axis of symmetry,

  iii A lies on the curve and has x-coordinate 9. Find its y-coordinate.

  iv B lies on the curve and has the same y-coordinate as A. Find length AB.

d The diagram shows the graph of $y = (x - 3)^2 - 16$

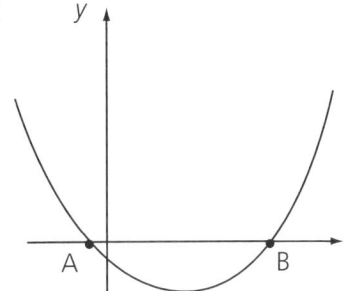

  i State the coordinates of the minimum turning point.

  ii State the equation of the axis of symmetry of the curve.

  iii B is the point (7, 0). Find the coordinates of A, the other x-axis intercept.

3 For each graph

  i Find the values of a and b.

  ii State the equation of the axis of symmetry.

  a graph $y = (x + a)^2 + b$ **b** graph $y = (x + a)^2 + b$ **c** graph $y = a - (x + b)^2$

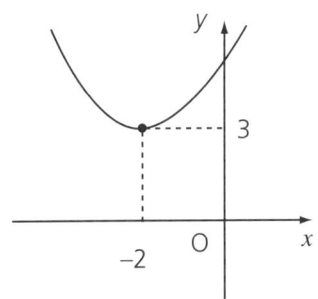

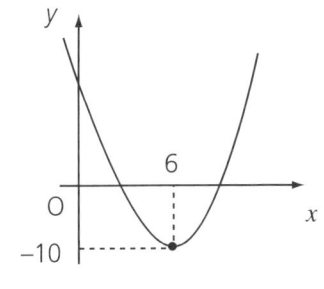

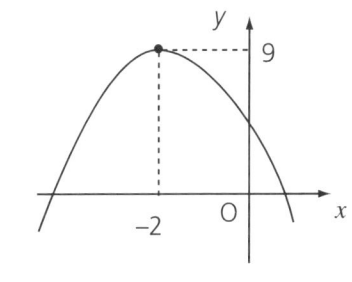

4 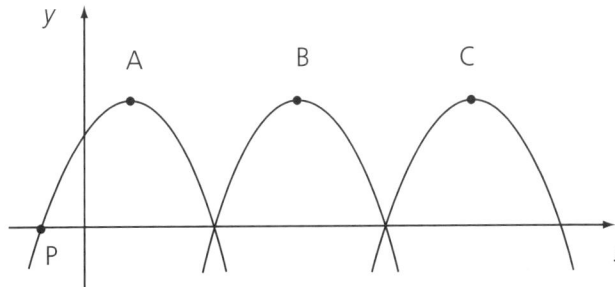 This parabola pattern consists of identical parabolas repeated. The first parabola, with maximum turning point A, has equation $y = 9 - (x - 1)^2$

  a State the coordinates of A

  b P is the point (−2, 0). Find the coordinates of B and C, the maximum turning points of the second and third parabolas.

11 Quadratic graphs and equations

Exercise 11b   Quadratic Equations: Solutions by Factorising

1. Solve these equations by first factorising the quadratic expression:

   a $x^2 + 2x - 15 = 0$ b $x^2 + 9x + 14 = 0$ c $x^2 - 6x + 5 = 0$

   d $x^2 - 8x + 16 = 0$ e $x^2 - 4x - 12 = 0$ f $x^2 - x - 12 = 0$

   g $2 - x - x^2 = 0$ h $12 - x - x^2 = 0$ i $10 - 3x - x^2 = 0$

2. For each graph:

   i   Find the coordinates of P and Q, the two x-axis intercepts

   ii   Find the equation of the axis of symmetry.

   a   graph $y = x^2 - 2x - 8$ b   graph $y = x^2 + 7x + 6$ 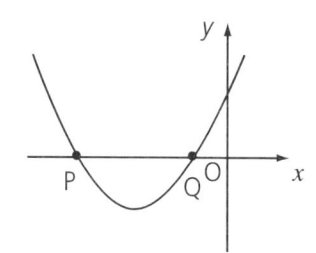   c   graph $y = 21 + 4x - x^2$

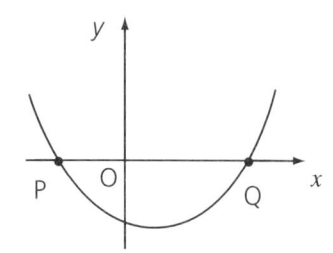

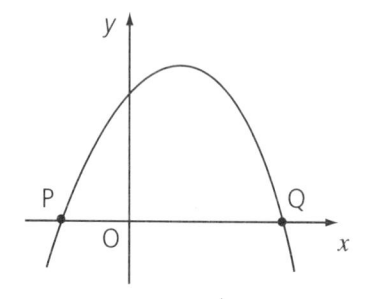

3. a   The diagram shows the graph $y = (x - 1)^2 - 4$

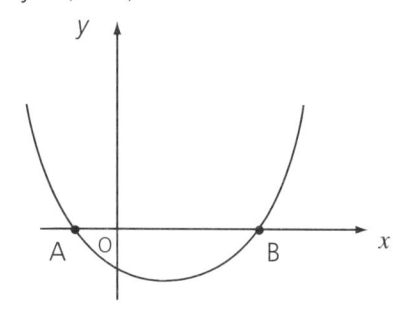

       i   Find the coordinates of the turning point.

       ii   Find the length AB.

   b   The diagram shows the graph $y = 25 - (x + 7)^2$

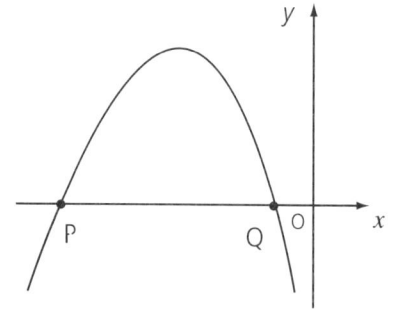

       i   Find the coordinates of the turning point.

       ii   Find the length PQ.

4. A rectangular garden consists of a rectangular patio area. The rest of the garden is a flowerbed as shown.

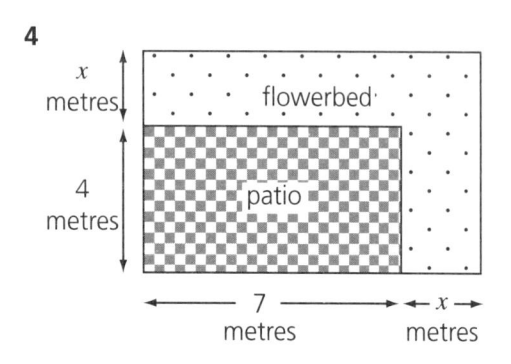

   a   State the length and breadth of the garden.

   b   Show that the area, A m², of the garden is given by the formula $A = x^2 + 11x + 28$

   c   The total area of the garden is 54 m². By making a quadratic equation and solving it find the dimensions of the garden.

See pages 42–46 of Leckie & Leckie's Intermediate 2 Maths Revision Notes

11 Quadratic graphs and equations

UNIT 3

Exercise 11c Quadratic Equations: Solutions by Formula

11.6

1. Use an appropriate formula to solve these quadratic equations, giving your answers correct to 1 decimal place:

   a $2x^2 - x - 8 = 0$
   b $x^2 + 3x - 2 = 0$
   c $3x^2 - 5x + 1 = 0$
   d $3x^2 + 4x - 5 = 0$
   e $x^2 - 2x - 10 = 0$
   f $3x^2 - 2x - 6 = 0$
   g $2x^2 + 3x - 1 = 0$
   h $2x^2 - 3x - 5 = 0$
   i $x^2 + 7x + 5 = 0$
   j $2p^2 - 5p - 4 = 0$
   k $6a^2 - 10a + 3 = 0$
   l $9y^2 + y - 2 = 0$

2. Find the roots of these equations correct to 1 decimal place:

   a $x^2 - x - 1 = 0$
   b $x^2 - 4x + 2 = 0$
   c $8x^2 + 3x - 1 = 0$

See Answers on pages 9–10 of answer booklet

12 Further trigonometry

12.1

Exercise 12a The Sine, Cosine and Tangent Graphs

1. On the same diagram sketch, for $0 \leqslant x \leqslant 360$, the graphs:

   a $y = \sin x°$ and $y = \cos x°$
   b $y = \sin x°$ and $y = \tan x°$
   c $y = \cos x°$ and $y = \tan x°$
   d $y = \sin x°$, $\cos x°$ and $\tan x°$

2. **a** The diagram shows $y = \sin x°$.
   b The diagram shows $y = \cos x°$.

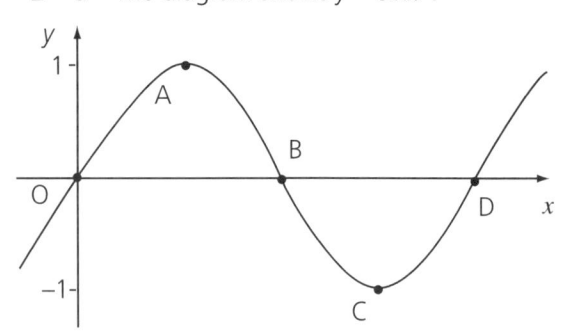

   State the coordinates of A, B, C and D.   State the coordinates of A, B, C, D and E.

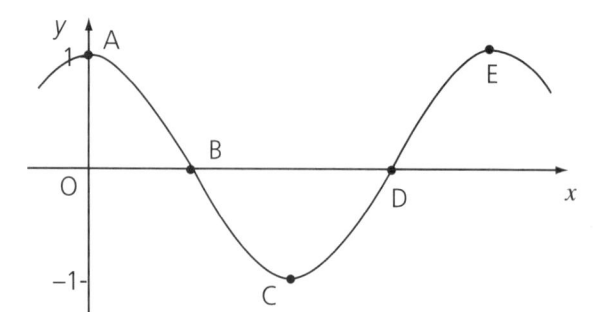

12.2

12.3

Exercise 12b Related Graphs

1. For each diagram, state the values of a and b:

   a graph of $y = a\sin bx°$ 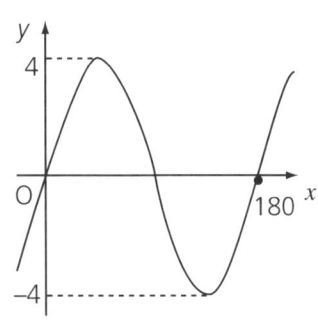
   b graph of $y = a\cos bx°$ 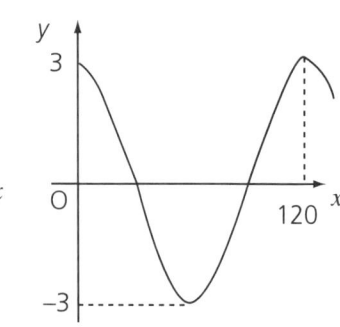
   c graph of $y = a\sin bx°$

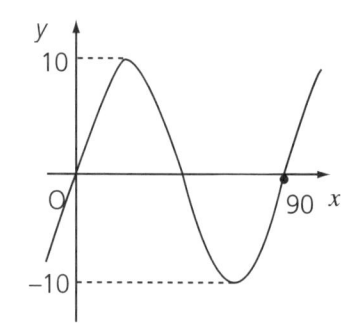

   d graph of $y = a\sin bx°$ 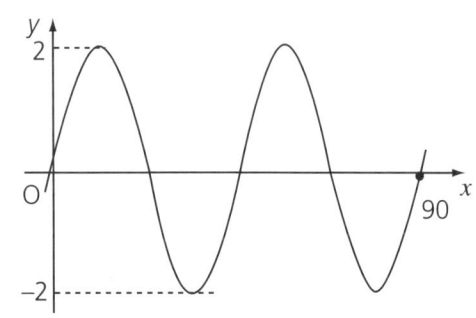
   e graph of $y = a\cos bx°$

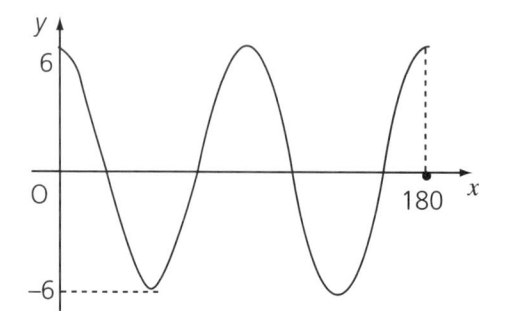

See pages 47–51 of Leckie & Leckie's Intermediate 2 Maths Revision Notes

12 Further trigonometry

UNIT 3

2 a The equation of this graph has the form $y = \cos(x - b)°$.
Find the value of b.

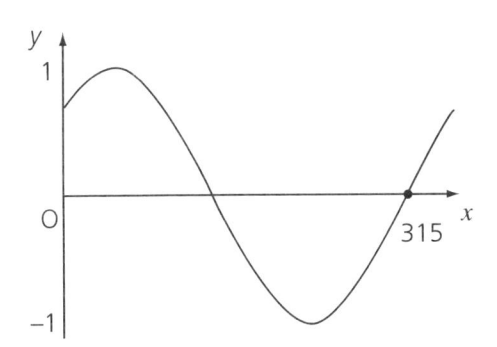

b The equation of this graph has the form $y = \cos(x + b)°$.
Find the value of b.

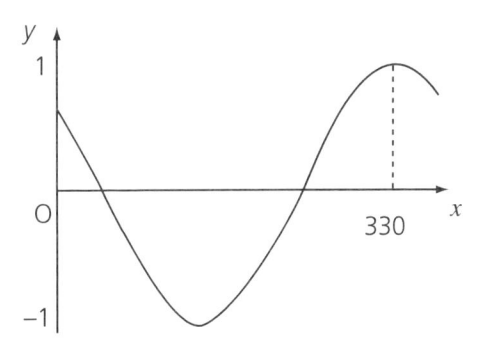

c The diagram shows the graph of $y = \sin(x - k)°$.
Find the value of k.

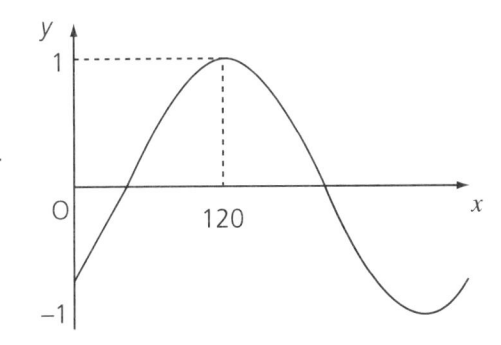

d The diagram shows the graph of $y = \sin(x + a)°$.
Find the value of a.

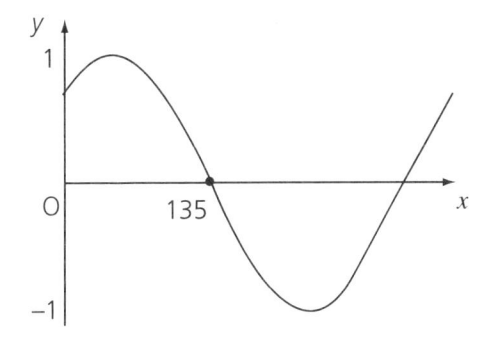

3 Sketch these graphs:

a $y = \cos 2x°$ for $0 \leqslant x \leqslant 360$

b $y = 4\sin x°$ for $0 \leqslant x \leqslant 360$

c $y = 3\sin 2x°$ for $0 \leqslant x \leqslant 360$

d $y = \sin(x - 45)°$ for $0 \leqslant x \leqslant 360$

e $y = \cos(x + 30)°$ for $0 \leqslant x \leqslant 360$

f $y = \cos(x + 60)°$ for $0 \leqslant x \leqslant 360$

See Answers on pages 10–11 of answer booklet

UNIT 3

12 Further trigonometry

12.4
12.5

Exercise 12c Solving Simple Trig Equations

1 a $y = \sin x°$

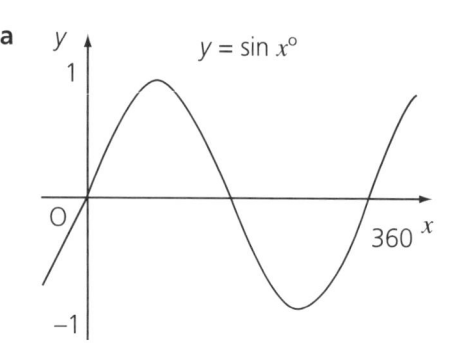

Use the graph to solve:
- i $\sin x° = 1$ $0 \leqslant x \leqslant 360$
- ii $\sin x° = 0$ $0 \leqslant x \leqslant 360$
- iii $\sin x° = 0$ $0 \leqslant x \leqslant 180$
- iv $\sin x° = -1$ $0 \leqslant x \leqslant 360$

b $y = \cos x°$

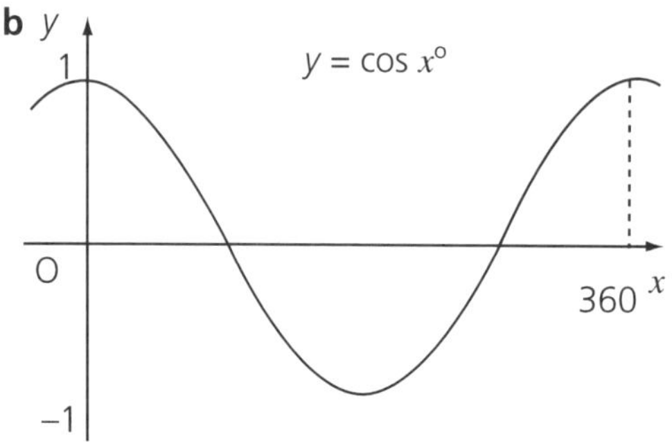

Use the graph to solve:
- i $\cos x° = 1$ $0 \leqslant x \leqslant 360$
- ii $\cos x° = 1$ $0 \leqslant x \leqslant 180$
- iii $\cos x° = -1$ $0 \leqslant x \leqslant 360$
- iv $\cos x° = 0$ $0 \leqslant x \leqslant 360$
- v $\cos x° = 0$ $0 \leqslant x \leqslant 180$

2 a The graph $y = \sin x°$ is shown. It is known that $\sin 30° = 0.5$.

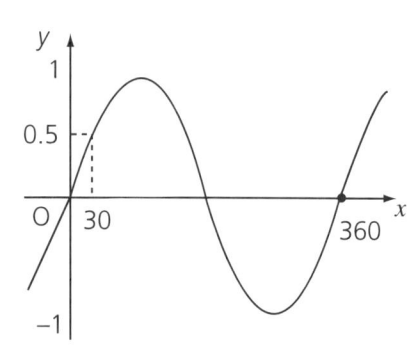

- i State another value of x for which $\sin x° = 0.5$, $0 \leqslant x \leqslant 360$
- ii State two values of x for which $\sin x° = -0.5$, $0 \leqslant x \leqslant 360$

b The graph $y = \cos x°$ is shown. It is known that $\cos 60° = 0.5$.

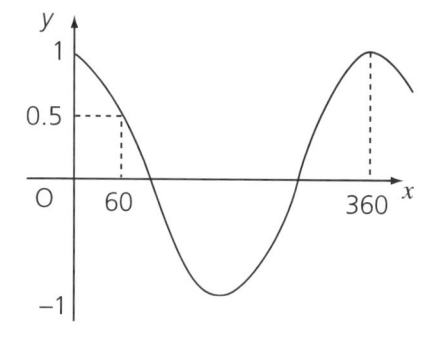

- i State another value of x for which $\cos x° = 0.5$, $0 \leqslant x \leqslant 360$
- ii State two values of x for which $\cos x° = -0.5$, $0 \leqslant x \leqslant 360$

3 a Given that $\sin 60° = 0.87$ (to 2 dec. places), what is the value of
- i $\sin 120°$
- ii $\sin 240°$
- iii $\sin 300°$?

b Given that $\cos 45° = 0.71$ (to 2 dec. places), what is the value of
- i $\cos 135°$
- ii $\cos 225°$
- iii $\cos 315°$?

c Given that $\tan 20° = 0.36$ (to 2 dec. places), what is the value of
- i $\tan 160°$
- ii $\tan 200°$
- iii $\tan 340°$?

See pages 47–51 of Leckie & Leckie's Intermediate 2 Maths Revision Notes

12 Further trigonometry — UNIT 3

4 Solve the following equations for $0 \leq x \leq 360$

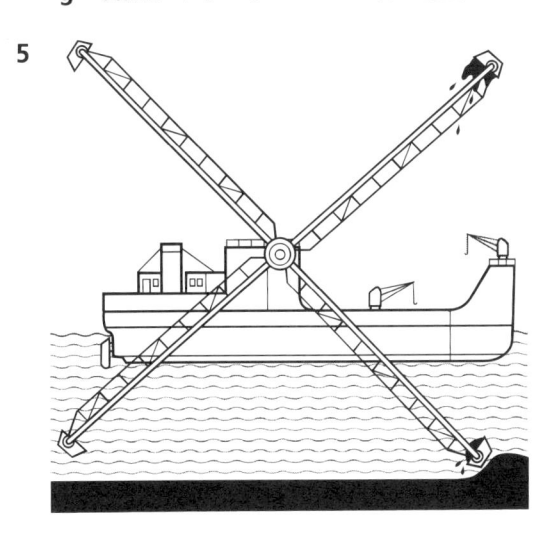

   a $3\sin x° - 2 = 0$ **b** $2\cos x° + 1 = 0$ **c** $7\tan x° + 12 = 0$

   d $3\tan x° - 5 = 0$ **e** $4\sin x° + 3 = 0$ **f** $5\cos x° - 2 = 0$

   g $6\tan x° + 5 = 1$ **h** $4\sin x° + 5 = 4$ **i** $9\cos x° + 7 = 5$

5 A dredger has four scoops on the end of 20-metre long rotating arms. The height, h metres, of one of the scoops above the silt, t seconds after start-up, is given by the formula
$h = 15 + 20\sin t°$

   a Find the height of the scoop above the silt after 50 seconds.

   b Find the times when the scoop enters and leaves the silt ($h = 0$) in the first rotation after start-up.

12.6 Exercise 12d Some Trig Formulae

1 Prove that:

   a $\cos^2 x° - \sin^2 x° = 2\cos^2 x° - 1$

   b $\dfrac{1 - \cos^2 A}{1 - \sin^2 A} = \tan^2 A°$

   c $1 - 2\sin^2 A = \cos^2 A - \sin^2 A$

   d $1 - \tan^2 x° = \dfrac{\cos^2 x° - \sin^2 x°}{\cos^2 x°}$

   e $\tan x° \sin x° = \dfrac{1 - \cos^2 x°}{\cos x°}$

   f $(\cos A - \sin A)^2 = 1 - 2\sin A \cos A$

2 Simplify:

   a $\cos^2 x° (\tan^2 x° + 1)$ **b** $\dfrac{\sin A}{\tan A}$ **c** $\tan^2 x° \cos^2 x°$

See Answers on page 11 of answer booklet

Exam Structure and Formulae

The current structure of assessment for the SQA Mathematics Intermediate 2 course consists of three Unit Assessments followed by the final Course Assessment.

The Unit Assessments

There are three of these, one for each Unit, assessing several outcomes based on the work of the particular Unit. For Unit 1 there are 5 outcomes, Unit 2 has 4 outcomes and Unit 3 has 3 outcomes. If a particular outcome is failed then you are allowed to be reassessed on just that outcome. The Unit Assessments are marked by your teacher.

The Course Exam

This is an 'External' exam marked by SQA markers and is usually sat sometime in May. There are two papers:

Paper 1 (non-calculator): 45 minutes
Paper 2 (calculator allowed): 1 hour 30 minutes

To gain a course award you must pass all three Unit Assessments as well as the final Course Exam.

Formulae list

The following formulae list is given to you in all your assessments.

The roots of $ax^2 + bx + c = 0$ are $x = \dfrac{-b \pm \sqrt{(b^2 - 4ac)}}{2a}$

Sine rule: $\dfrac{a}{\sin A} = \dfrac{b}{\sin B} = \dfrac{c}{\sin C}$

Cosine rule: $a^2 = b^2 + c^2 - 2bc \cos A$ or $\cos A = \dfrac{b^2 + c^2 - a^2}{2bc}$

Area of a triangle: Area $= \tfrac{1}{2}ab \sin C$

Volume of a sphere: Volume $= \tfrac{4}{3}\pi r^3$

Volume of a cone: Volume $= \tfrac{1}{3}\pi r^2 h$

Volume of a cylinder: Volume $= \pi r^2 h$

Standard deviation: $s = \sqrt{\dfrac{\sum(x - \bar{x})^2}{n - 1}} = \sqrt{\dfrac{\sum x^2 - (\sum x)^2/n}{n - 1}}$, where n is the sample size

Unit Assessments

Practice assessment A for Unit 1

Outcome 1

1. £540 is invested for two years at 5% compound interest per annum. How much interest would be paid on this investment?

2. A car is bought for £13,500. It depreciates by 18% after one year and by 7% after the second year. Calculate the value of the car after the two years.

Outcome 2

3. Calculate the volume of the cone shown in the diagram.

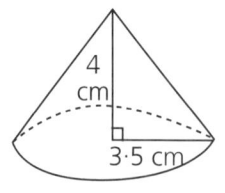

4. 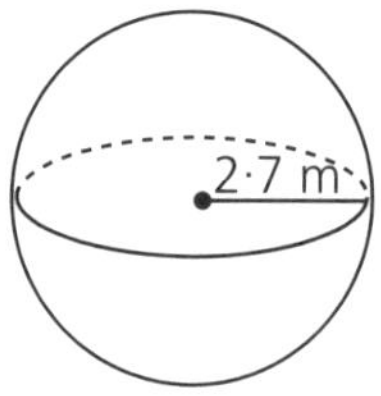 Calculate, to two significant figures, the volume of a sphere with radius 2·7 m.

5. A soup can is in the shape of a cylinder with radius 4·2 cm and height 9·5 cm. Calculate the volume of the can correct to three significant figures.

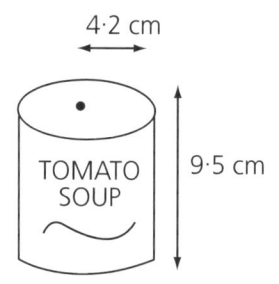

Outcome 3

6. A is the point (−1, −3) and B is the point (7, 2). Find the gradient of the line AB.

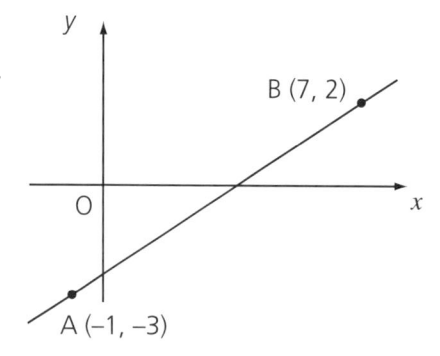

7. Sketch the line $y = 3x - 4$, showing clearly the coordinates of the y-axis intercept.

8. Find the equation of the straight line graph shown in the diagram.

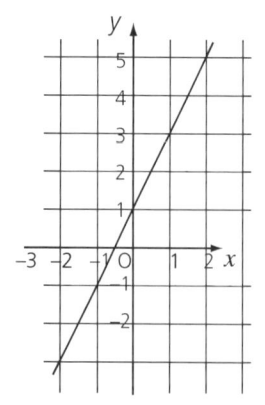

See pages 3-20 of Leckie & Leckie's Intermediate 2 Maths Revision Notes

Practice assessment A for Unit 1

Outcome 4

9 a Simplify $a(5a - b)$ **b** Simplify $(x - 3)(x + 2)$

10 Factorise:

   a $8x - x^2$ **b** $m^2 - n^2$ **c** $x^2 + 4x - 21$

Outcome 5

11 Calculate the length of arc AB in this circle: (65°, 18 cm)

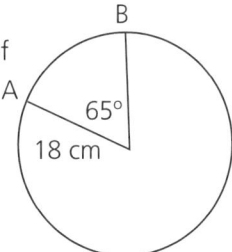

12 Calculate the area of the shaded sector in this circle: (115°, 5·3 cm)

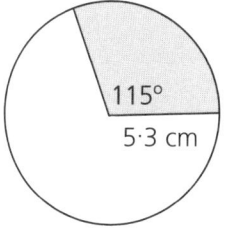

13 AB and AD are tangents to the circle centre C, making a kite ABCD as shown, with angle BCD = 145°.

   a State the size of angle ABC.

   b Find the size of angle BAD.

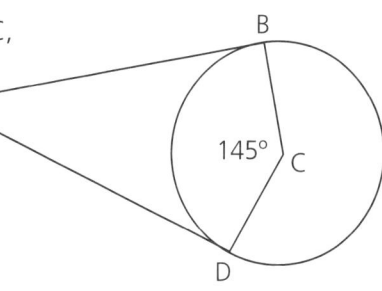

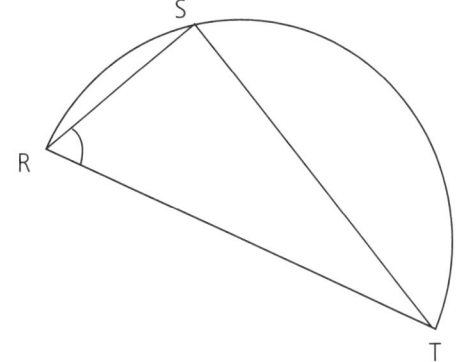

14 The diagram shows a triangle RST inscribed in a semicircle with diameter RT. Angle STR = 22°. Find the size of the marked angle.

Practice assessment B for Unit 1

Outcome 1

1. Multimoney offers a rate of 8% compound interest per annum on investments. If £930 is invested with Multimoney for two years, how much interest would this pay?

2. During its first year a brand new £16500 car depreciates by 17%. During its second year it depreciates a further 9%. What is the car worth after two years?

Outcome 2

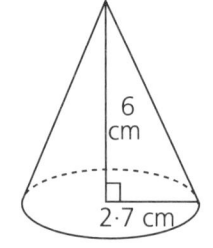

3. Calculate the volume of this cone. (height 6 cm, base radius 2·7 cm)

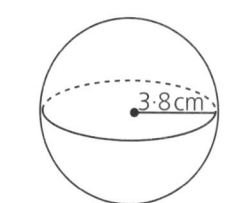

4. Calculate, to two significant figures, the volume of this sphere with radius 3·8 cm.

5. This oil drum is in the shape of a cylinder with base radius 1·8 m and height 2·3 m. Calculate the volume of the drum correct to 3 significant figures.

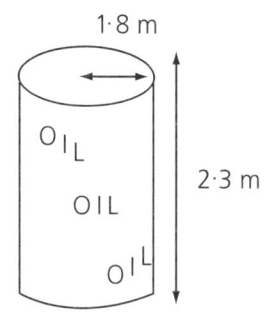

Outcome 3

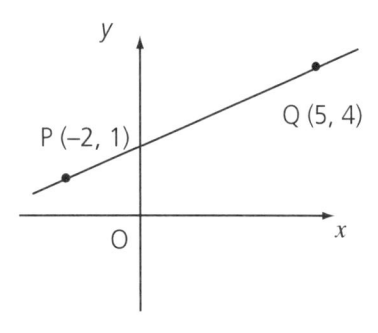

6. P is the point (−2, 1) and Q is the point (5, 4). Find the gradient of the line PQ.

7. Sketch the graph of the line $y = 2x - 3$, showing clearly the coordinates of the y-axis intercept.

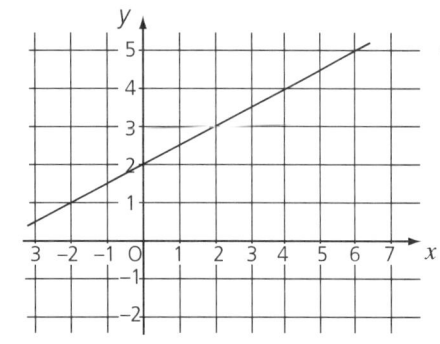

8. Find the equation of the straight line graph shown in this diagram.

See pages 3–20 of Leckie & Leckie's Intermediate 2 Maths Revision Notes

Practice assessment B for Unit 1

Outcome 4

9 Simplify:

   a $m(8m + n)$　　　　**b** $(a - 5)(a - 6)$

10 Factorise:

   a $y^2 + 3y - 10$　　**b** $2mn - m^2$　　**c** $p^2 - q^2$

Outcome 5

11 Calculate the length of arc RS in this circle with radius 23 cm.

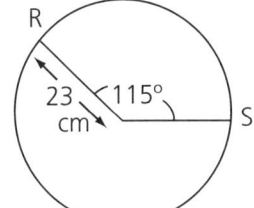

12 Calculate the area of the shaded sector in this circle.

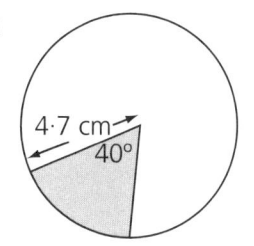

13 From the point T, two tangents TS and TU have been drawn to the circle centre V. The shape TSVU is a tangent kite. Angle SVU = 155°. Find the size of:

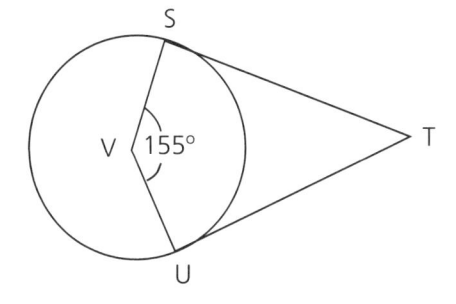

   a angle VST.

   b angle STU.

14 The diagram shows a semicircle with diameter MQ with an inscribed triangle MNQ. Angle QMN = 18°.
Find the size of the marked angle NQM.

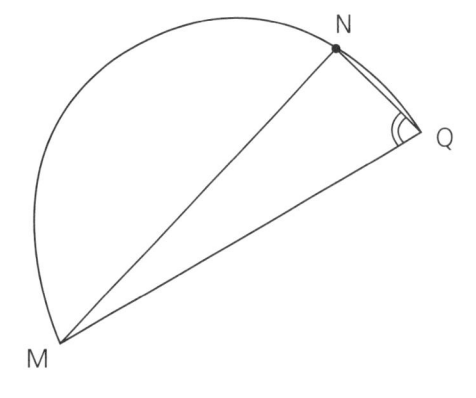

Practice assessment A for Unit 2

Outcome 1

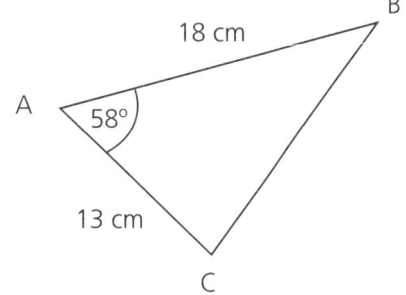

1 A triangular piece of wood is shown.

    a Calculate the area of the piece of wood.

    b Calculate the length of side BC. (Do not use a scale drawing.)

2 The diagram shows two television detector vans positioned at P and Q. A television is detected at A, 23 metres from P. If angle QPA = 43° and angle PQA = 88° calculate the distance of the television at A from the detector van at Q.

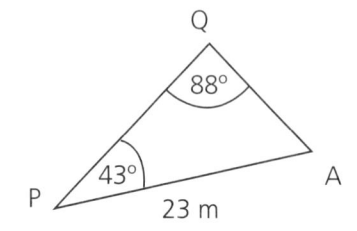

Outcome 2

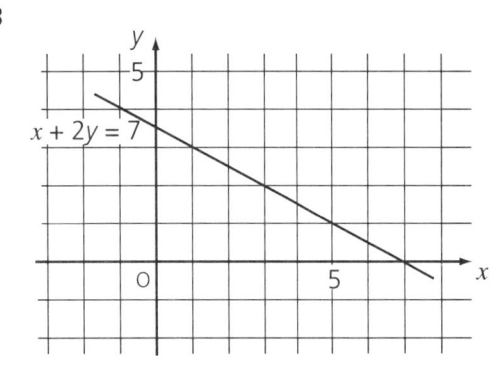

3 This diagram shows the graph of the line $x + 2y = 7$

    a On the same diagram draw the straight line graph $y + x = 5$.

    b Use your graph to solve the system of equations:

    $x + 2y = 7$
    $y + x = 5$.

4 Solve, algebraically, the system of equations:

$6x - y = 1$

$2x + 3y = 17$.

See pages 21–36 of Leckie & Leckie's Intermediate 2 Maths Revision Notes

Practice assessment A for Unit 2

Outcome 3

5 The heights of 14 seedlings were recorded. (Measurements were in millimetres.)

45, 65, 35, 49, 36, 56, 38, 56, 57, 40, 51, 52, 38, 51

   a Find the maximum, minimum, median and upper and lower quartiles for this data set.

   b Draw a boxplot to illustrate this data.

6 A medical survey was done involving 50 school pupils concerning weight. This table gives the results:

Category	Number of pupils	Angle at centre
Underweight	8	
Normal	27	
Overweight	15	

   a Complete the 'Angle at centre' column to help you plan a piechart drawing of the data.

   b Draw a piechart to illustrate the data.

Outcome 4

7 Use an appropriate formula to calculate the standard deviation of this data set:

8, 4, 7, 7, 10, 9

Show all necessary working.

8 This scattergraph shows the twelve monthly average temperatures in Country B plotted against those of Country A.

   a Draw an approximate line of best fit for this scattergraph.

   b Find the equation of this line.

   c Use this equation to estimate the average monthly temperature in Country B for a month with average 12°C in Country A.

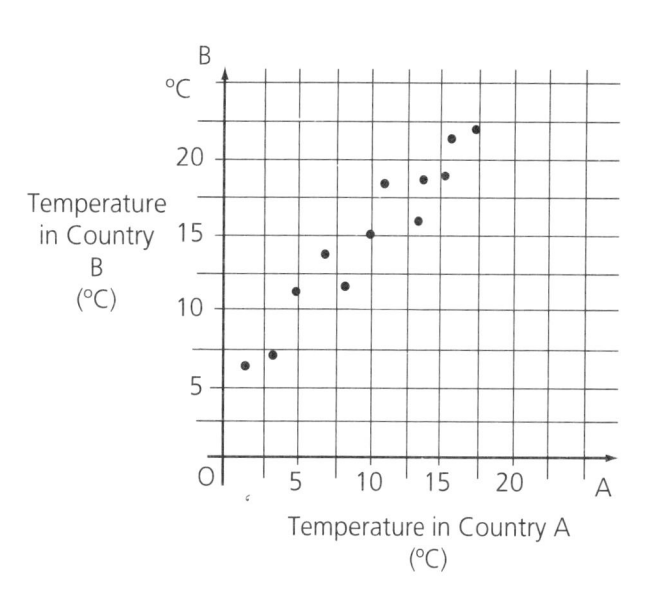

9 A number is chosen at random from the numbers 1 to 50. What is the probability that it is less than 12?

Practice assessment B for Unit 2

Outcome 1

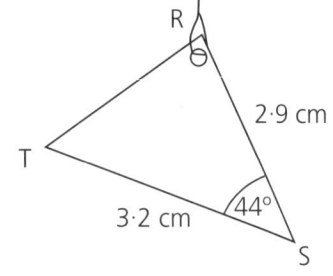

1. The diagram shows a triangular pendant.

   a Calculate the area of pendant.

   b Calculate the length of side RT. (Do not use a scale drawing.)

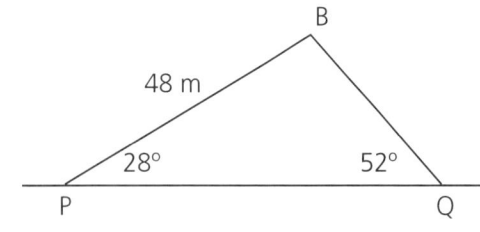

2. The diagram shows the position of a balloon at B as seen by two observers, one at P and one at Q. The balloon is 48 m from observer P. If angle BPQ = 28° and angle PQB = 52° calculate the distance of the balloon from observer Q.

Outcome 2

3. The diagram shows the graph of the line $2x + 3y = 14$.

   a On the same diagram draw the straight line graph $y = 3x + 1$.

   b Use your graph to solve the system of equations:

   $2x + 3y = 14$

   $y = 3x + 1$.

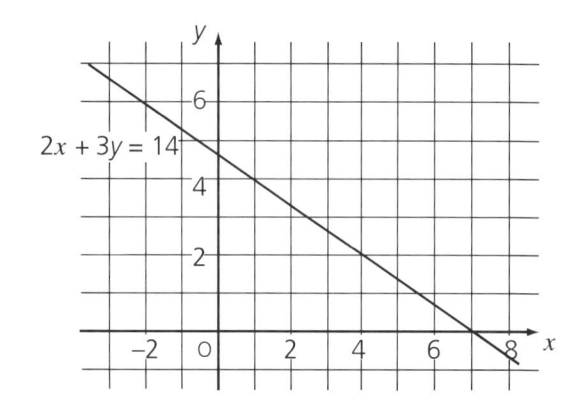

4. Solve, algebraically, the system of equations:

   $3x + 4y = 29$

   $2x - y = 1$.

Outcome 3

5. 22 pupils were timed during a maths test to see how long they took to complete it. The times, in minutes, were:

   15, 30, 26, 21, 23, 30, 27, 24, 16, 6, 18

   24, 21, 15, 14, 30, 16, 24, 21, 26, 23, 20

   a Find the maximum, minimum, median and upper and lower quartiles for this data set.

   b Draw a boxplot to illustrate this data.

See pages 21–36 of Leckie & Leckie's Intermediate 2 Maths Revision Notes

Practice assessment B for Unit 2

6 A survey of the 65 audience members immediately after a show at the local theatre revealed the following concerning what they thought of the length of the show:

Category	Number of audience members	Angle at centre
Too short	18	
About right	33	
Too long	14	

    a Complete the 'Angle at centre' column to help you plan a piechart diagram of the data.

    b Draw a piechart to illustrate the data.

Outcome 4

7 Use an appropriate formula to calculate the standard deviation of this data set, showing all necessary working:

4, 8, 3, 7, 7

8 The prices of 13 articles in two different European countries were compared. The results, in Euros, are shown in this scattergraph

    a Draw an your best estimate of the line of best fit on the scattergraph.

    b Find the equation of the line.

    c Use the equation to estimate the probable cost in Country B of an article costing €9 in Country A.

9 A number is chosen at random from 1 to 29. What is the probability that it is greater than 24?

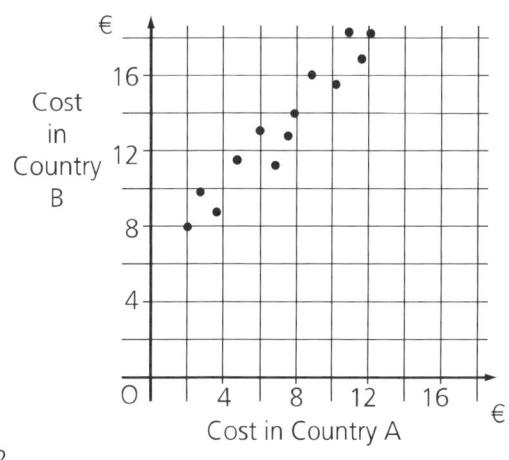

Practice assessment A for Unit 3

Outcome 1

1. Simplify $\dfrac{(2a-3)(a+1)}{(2a-3)^2}$, $a \neq \dfrac{3}{2}$

2. Simplify

   a $\dfrac{12}{m} + \dfrac{3}{m}$ b $\dfrac{2}{a} - \dfrac{3}{b}$ c $\dfrac{4x}{y} \times \dfrac{z}{3}$ d $\dfrac{m}{n} \div \dfrac{k}{5}$

3. Change the subject of the formula $y = ax + b$ to x.

4. Simplify

   a $\sqrt{27}$ b $\sqrt{\dfrac{81}{16}}$

5. Simplify

   a $\dfrac{x^9 \times x^5}{x^3}$ b $3m^{-2} \times 4m^4$

Outcome 2

6. The diagram shows the graph $y = kx^2$. Find the value of k and hence write down the equation.

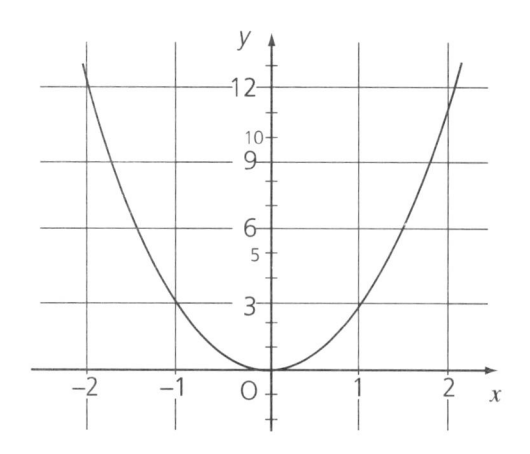

7. The diagram shows a graph of the form $y = (x + a)^2 + b$. Find the values of a and b and hence write down the equation of the graph.

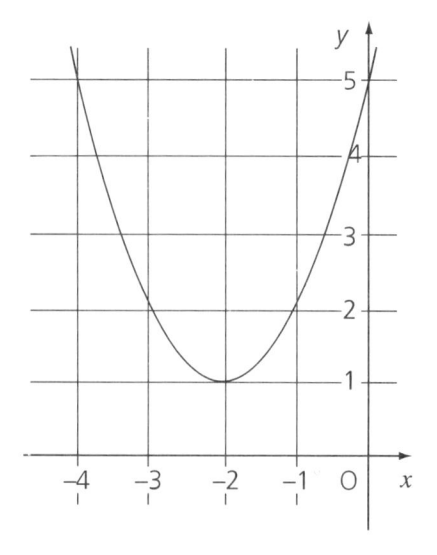

See pages 37–51 of Leckie & Leckie's Intermediate 2 Maths Revision Notes

Practice assessment A for Unit 3

8 A quadratic function has equation $y = (x + 2)^2 - 3$.

   a Write down the equation of the axis of symmetry of its graph.

   b Write down the coordinates of the turning point of the graph of this function and state whether it is a maximum of a minimum.

9 The diagram shows the graph with equation $y = x^2 + 4x + 3$. Use the graph to solve the equation $x^2 + 4x + 3 = 0$

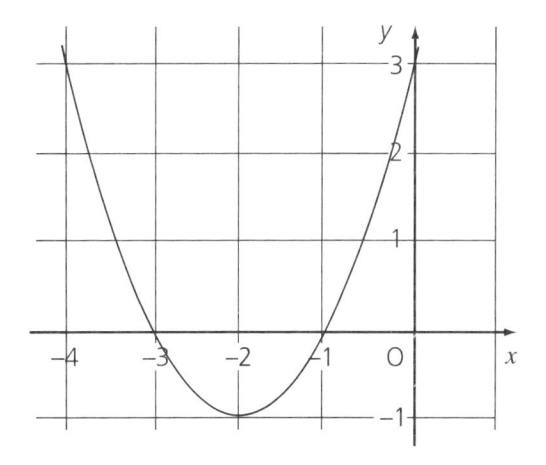

10 Use factorisation to solve $x^2 - 2x - 35 = 0$

11 Use the quadratic formula to solve $x^2 + 3x - 6 = 0$

Outcome 3

12 Sketch the graph of $y = \cos 4x°$ for $0 \leqslant x \leqslant 360$

13 The diagram shows a graph of the form $y = \cos bx°$.

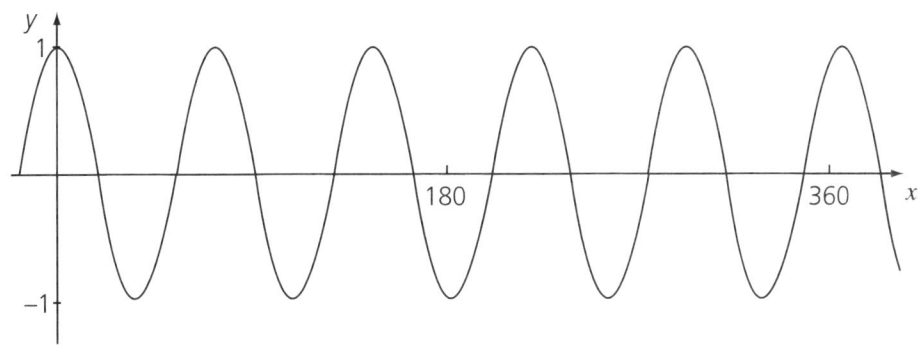

Write down the value of b.

14 Solve $4\cos x° + 3 = 0$ for $0 \leqslant x \leqslant 360$.

Practice assessment B for Unit 3

Outcome 1

1. Simplify $\dfrac{(x+1^2)}{(x+1)(x-2)}$, $x \neq -1$, $x \neq 2$

2. Simplify

   a $\dfrac{5}{x} + \dfrac{7}{x}$ b $\dfrac{11}{m} - \dfrac{6}{n}$ c $\dfrac{3x}{y} \times \dfrac{2}{k}$ d $\dfrac{a}{b} \div \dfrac{c}{5}$

3. Change the subject of the formula $A = B + Cx$ to x.

4. Simplify

   a $\sqrt{54}$ b $\sqrt{\dfrac{100}{49}}$

5. Simplify

   a $\dfrac{m^{12} \times m^{-1}}{m^3}$ b $7x^{\frac{1}{2}} \times 3x^{\frac{3}{2}}$

Outcome 2

6. The diagram shows a graph of the form $y = kx^2$.
   Determine the value of k and hence write down the equation of the graph.

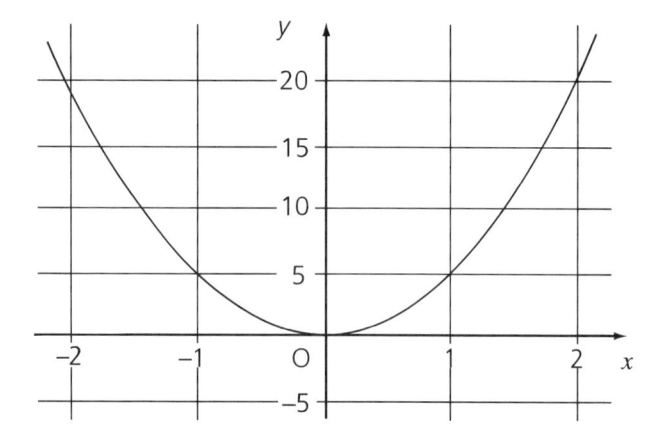

7. The diagram shows a graph with equation of the form $y = (x + a)^2 + b$.
   Find the values of a and b and hence write down the equation.

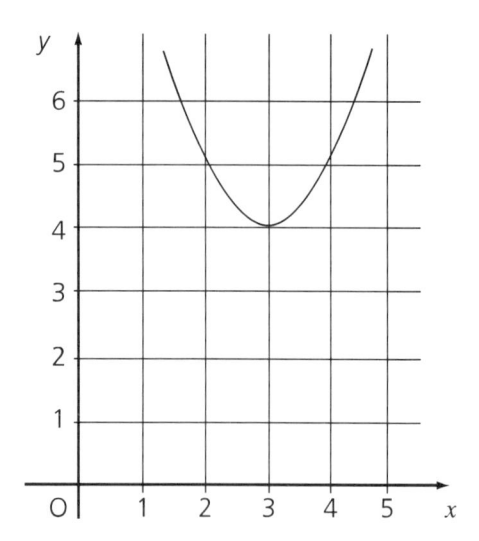

See pages 37–51 of Leckie & Leckie's Intermediate 2 Maths Revision Notes

Practice assessment B for Unit 3

8 A quadratic function has equation $y = (x - 5)^2 + 2$.

   a Write down the equation of the axis of symmetry of the graph of this function.

   b Write down the coordinates of the turning point of the graph of this function and state whether it is a maximum of a minimum.

9 The diagram shows the graph of the quadratic function $y = x^2 - 3x - 4$. Use the graph to solve the equation
$x^2 - 3x - 4 = 0$

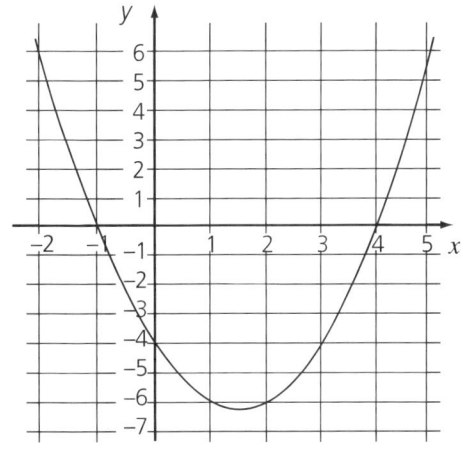

10 Use factorisation to solve $x^2 - 8x + 15 = 0$

11 Use the quadratic formula to solve $x^2 - 5x - 8 = 0$

Outcome 3

12 Sketch the graph of $y = \sin 4x°$ for $0 \leqslant x \leqslant 360$

13 The diagram shows the graph with equation of the form $y = \sin bx°$.

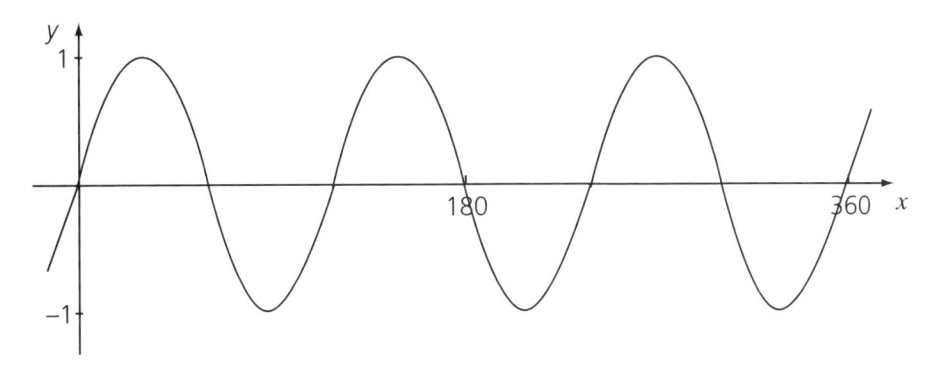

Write down the value of b.

14 Solve $3\sin x° - 1 = 0$ for $0 \leqslant x \leqslant 360$.

Course Assessments

Practice Course Exam A

Paper 1 (Non-calculator) *Time allowed: 45 minutes*

1 a Find the equation of the straight line shown in the diagram.

b Find the coordinates of the point where the line $y = x + 3$ meets this line.

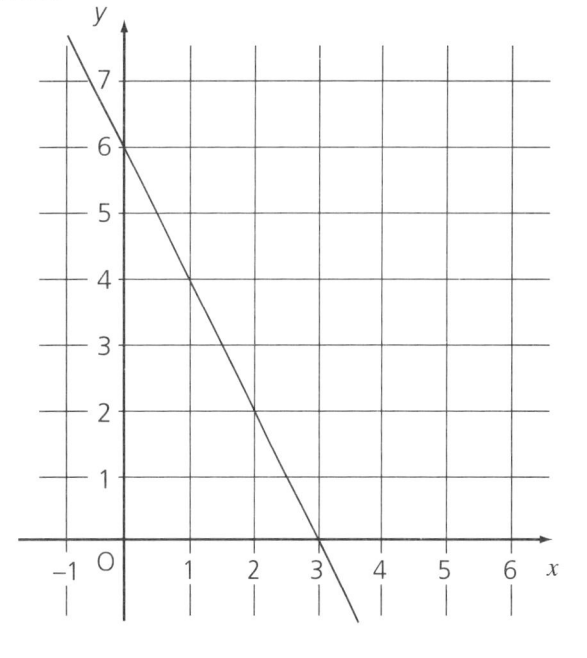

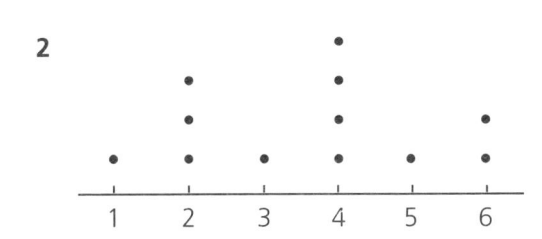

2 This dotplot shows the time taken, in minutes, for 12 pupils to get from one class to the next class. What is the probability that one of these pupils, chosen at random took longer than 4 minutes?

3 a Multiply out the brackets and collect like terms:
$3a + (2a - 1)(a - 3)$

b Factorise $3x^2 + 14x - 5$

4 The lifespans of 14 ants were recorded. The results are shown in this stem and leaf diagram:

a For this data calculate:
  i the median
  ii the lower quartile
  iii the upper quartile

b Construct a boxplot for the data.

c Similar data for a different species of ant produced the same value for the median. The semi-interquartile range for this second sample was 2·5. Make an appropriate comment about the lifespans of the two species.

```
3 | 3 9
4 | 2 2 6 8
5 | 2 4 4 4 5 5
6 | 0 5
```

n = 14   4 | 2 represents 42 days

Practice Course Exam A

5 BT is a tangent to the circle, centre C, with point of contact T. Line BC extends to meet the circle at D. Angle CBT = 25°. Calculate the size of angle CDT.

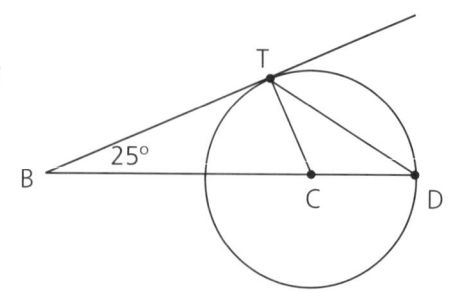

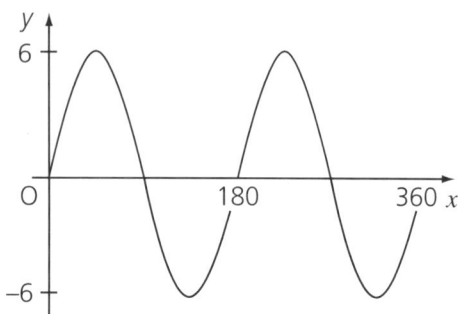

6 The diagram shows the graph of $y = k\sin ax°$. State the values of k and a.

7 The diagram shows the graph of $y = (x + 2)^2 - 1$

   a Write down the coordinates of the minimum turning point.

   b State the equation of the axis of symmetry.

   c Line AB is parallel to the x-axis with B being the y-axis intercept of the parabola. Find the coordinates of point A.

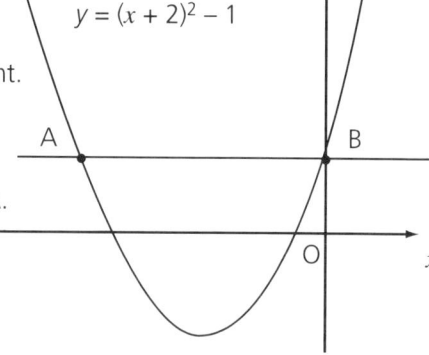

8 Simplify $\dfrac{3a^{-\frac{1}{2}} \times 2a^{\frac{3}{2}}}{a^2}$

Paper 2 (Calculator allowed) *Time allowed: 1 hour 30 minutes*

1 At 7.00 pm a bacteria culture contained 1000 bacteria. The number of bacteria increased at the rate of 2% per minute. How many bacteria were there at 7.04pm?

2 A sample of 4-week-old mice was weighed. Their weights, in grams, were as follows:
13, 14, 13, 12, 16, 13.

   a Calculate:

      i   the mean   ii   the standard deviation

   of these weights. Show clearly all your working.

   b The same six mice were again weighed 1 week later. Each had gained 4 grams. For the new weights write down:

      i   the mean   ii   the standard deviation

   c After a further 1 week it was noticed that the standard deviation had increased a lot compared with previously. Make an appropriate comment about the distribution of the weights about the mean weight compared to the previous weighings.

3 A school offers pupils two types of calculators to buy: a basic model and a scientific model.

   a Class 2B's order came to a total of £55 and consisted of 3 basic calculators and 5 scientific calculators. Let £x be the cost of a basic calculator and £y be the cost of a scientific calculator. Write down an equation that represents 2B's order.

   b Class 2C ordered 2 basic and 7 scientific calculators at a cost of £66. Write down a second equation, this time to represent 2C's order.

   c Calculate the cost of a basic calculator and of a scientific calculator.

Practice Course Exam A

4 The diagram shows the layout of a discus throwing circle.
The diameter of the circle is 2·5 m.
Calculate the area of the shaded sector.

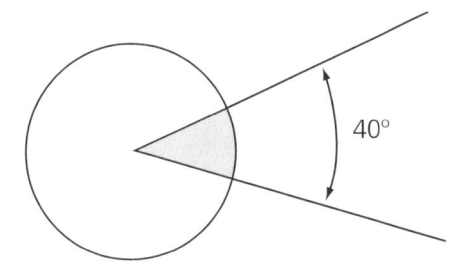

5 Rock R lies 40 m from lighthouse L on a bearing of 048°. Rock S lies 62 m from lighthouse L on a bearing 073°.

    a Calculate the size of angle RLS.

    b Calculate the distance between the two rocks R and S. (Do not use a scale drawing.)

    c Calculate the area of sea contained within triangle LRS.

6 Solve the equation $7x^2 - 5x - 2 = 0$, giving the roots correct to 1 decimal place.

7 A luxury chocolate manufacturer produces spherical and conical sweets.
The sphere has diameter 2·8 cm.
The cone has a base diameter that is also 2·8 cm.

    a Calculate the volume of the spherical chocolate.
Give your answer correct to two significant figures.

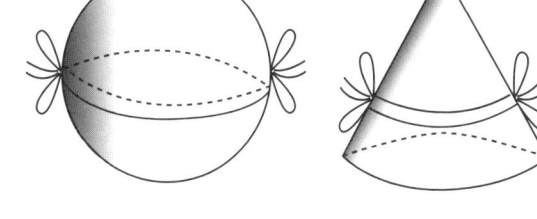

    b If the conical chocolate has the same volume as the spherical chocolate, calculate the height of the cone.

8 The diagram shows a square with side $2x$ cm with a $(x - 1)$ cm by $(x + 1)$ cm rectangle removed from it.
Show that the area, A cm², of the resulting shape is given by the formula $A = 3x^2 + 1$.

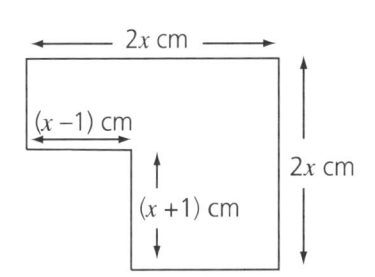

9 a Simplify

      i $\sqrt{50} - \sqrt{18}$ **ii** $\dfrac{2a}{b} \div \dfrac{a^2}{3}$

   b Change the subject of the formula $V = 2xy + 6$ to x.

10 a Solve the equation $5\tan x° + 9 = 0$ for $0 \leqslant x \leqslant 360$.

    b Simplify $1 - \cos^2 x° \tan^2 x°$.

Practice Course Exam B

Paper 1 (Non-calculator) *Time allowed: 45 minutes*

1 A die is rolled at the same time as a coin is tossed.

	1	2	3	4	5	6
Head	H, 1	H, 2				
Tail	T, 1					

    a Complete the table to show all the possible outcomes.

    b What is the probability that a number greater than 2 is rolled along with the coin showing a head?

2 Multiply out the brackets and collect like terms:

$(5x - 2y)(x - 3y)$

3 The diagram shows a straight line graph.

    a Find the equation of the graph.

    b State the coordinates of the x-axis intercept of the graph.

4 Sketch the graph $y = 2\cos 2x$ for $\leqslant x \leqslant 360$.

5 A sample of hens' eggs was weighed with the following results. The weights are in grams.

53, 58, 60, 55, 59, 53, 57, 48, 51, 62, 57, 64, 61, 50, 60, 56, 50

    a Find median and lower and upper quartiles for this data.

    b Construct a boxplot for the data.

    c A further sample was weighed after a new feed was given to the hens. Here is the boxplot from the new data.

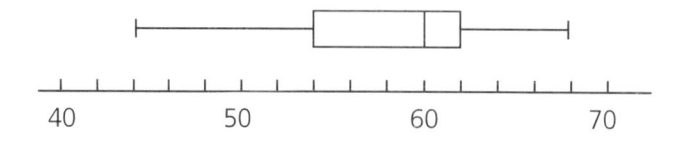

Compare the two boxplots and comment on the effectiveness of the new feed.

Practice Course Exam B

6 The diagram shows the graph with equation $y = 1 - (x - 2)^2$.

   a Write down the coordinates of the maximum turning point.

   b State the equation of the axis of symmetry of the graph.

   c The graph cuts the x-axis at the points A and B. Find the coordinates of these two points. Show clearly all your working.

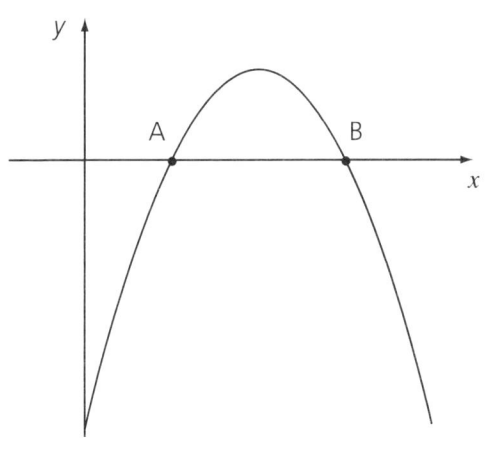

7 **a** Express $\dfrac{5}{\sqrt{2}}$ as a fraction with a rational denominator.

   b Simplify $\dfrac{2}{a} - \dfrac{3}{a^2}$.

8 The diagrams show a circular cross-section of a cylindrical water tank. The radius OB is 3 metres. The depth of water from the bottom of the tank to the water's surface AB is 5 metres.

Calculate the width, w metres, of the water surface in the tank.

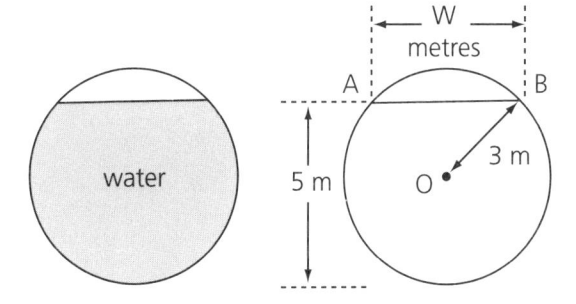

Paper 2 (Calculator allowed) *Time allowed: 1 hour 30 minutes*

1 A large city hospital recorded the ages of admissions to their casualty department for a Saturday evening. The results are shown in the table:

Construct a pie chart to illustrate this information. Show all your working.

Age	No. of admissions
0–15	2
16–18	21
19–21	28
Over 21	9

2 Solve algebraically the system of equations
$2x - 3y = 15$
$3x + 2y = 3$

3 For the circle shown in the diagram:
- ST is a diameter
- WT is a tangent
- VU is parallel to WT.

If angle WTU = 40° calculate the size of angle SUV.

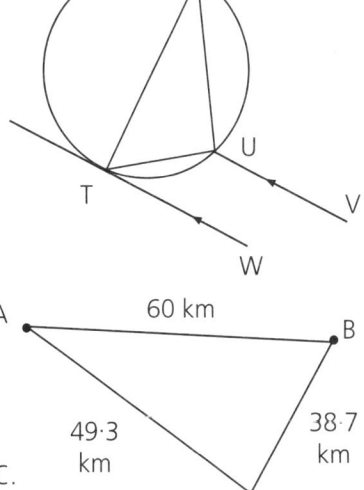

4 The diagram shows the relative positions and distances of three ships A, B and C at sea.

   a Calculate the size of angle A.

   b Calculate the area of sea enclosed by triangle ABC.

Practice Course Exam B

5 At an ostrich farm egg weights were recorded using a random sample of ten eggs. The weights, in kilograms, are:

1·8, 1·4, 1·5, 2·1, 1·8, 1·3, 1·5, 1·5 1·6, 1·5

For this data, $\Sigma x = 16$ and $\Sigma x^2 = 26·1$ where x is the weight, in kg, of an egg.

   a Calculate the mean weight of the ten eggs.

   b Using an appropriate formula, calculate the standard deviation for this data, giving your answer to two significant figures.

   c A new feed is given to the ostriches. After two months, a further sample of ten eggs was weighed. For this new sample:
   mean weight (kg) = 1·7 kg   standard deviation = 0·63
   Comment, with reasons, on the effect of the new feed on egg weight.

6 A hemispherical bowl with radius 12 cm is filled with water from cylindrical glasses with base radius 3 cm and height 10 cm.

   a Calculate the volume of the bowl.

   b How many glasses fill the bowl?
   (Show clearly all your working.)

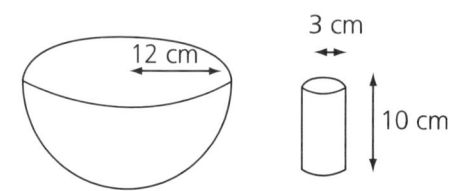

7 a i Factorise $a^2 - 9$.

   ii Factorise $a^2 - a - 6$

   iii Hence express $\dfrac{a^2-9}{a^2-a-6}$ in its simplest form.

   b Change the subject of the formula $A = \pi r^2 + 3$ to r.

8 Assume the Earth makes a circular orbit of the sun with a radius of approximately 150 million km.

Calculate the distance travelled by the Earth along it's orbit from position A to position B as shown in the diagram.

9 Solve the equation $3x^2 - 6x + 2 = 0$ giving your answers correct to one decimal place.

10 a Simplify $10y^{\frac{3}{2}} \div 2y^{-\frac{1}{2}}$.

   b Evaluate this expression when $y = 4$.

11 A tyre is being tested by the manufacturers on an artificial road surface. A mark is made on the tyre at position A shown in the diagram. The height, H cm, of the mark above the 'road surface' is given by the formula $H = 30 + 30\sin t°$ where t is the time in thousandths of a second after the start of the test.

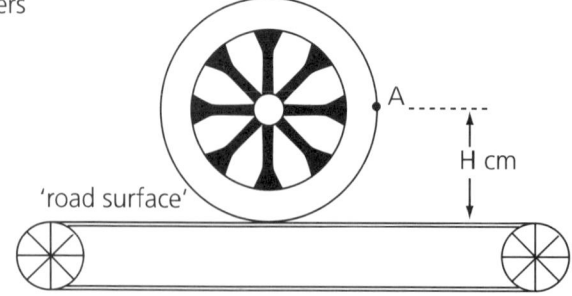

   a Find the height of the mark after 90 thousandths of a second.

   b Find the <u>two</u> times during the first turn of the tyre when the mark on the tyre is 40 cm above the road surface.